"This volume offers thoughtful and sometimes provocative reflection on contextual theology for our era. Contextual theology is both critiqued and affirmed as the authors, who span a range of continents and contexts, wrestle with just how theology can be in dialogue with daily life. New agendas for engaging with culture, Christology, and theological education are also suggested. This collection of essays is indeed a stimulating and challenging read."

—CATHY ROSS
Tutor in Contextual Theology, Ripon College, Cuddesdon, Oxford

"Christians in the twenty-first-century must no longer engage in mission or do theology that is not faithful to Christ and relevant to their context. Steve Bevans's illuminating essays accompanied by other voices should be heard as important steps as we join God's missional journey in this century. With some critique of the past and hope for the future we are reminded that contextual theology has never been more important for our understanding and practice of mission."

—DARRELL WHITEMAN
Vice President of The Mission Society, and former Professor and Dean of the E. Stanley Jones School of World Mission and Evangelism, Asbury Theological Seminary

Contextual Theology for the Twenty-First Century

Missional Church, Public Theology, World Christianity

Stephen Bevans, Paul S. Chung, Veli-Matti Kärkkäinen
and Craig L. Nessan, Series Editors

IN THE MIDST OF globalization there is crisis as well as opportunity. A model of God's mission is of special significance for ecclesiology and public theology when explored in diverse perspectives and frameworks in the postcolonial context of World Christianity. In the face of the new, complex global civilization characterized by the Second Axial Age, the theology of mission, missional ecclesiology, and public ethics endeavor to provide a larger framework for missiology in interaction with our social, multicultural, political, economic, and intercivilizational situation; they create ways to refurbish mission as constructive theology in critical and creative engagement with cultural anthropology, world religions, prophetic theology, postcolonial hermeneutics, and contextual theologies of World Christianity. Such endeavors play a critical role in generating theological, missional, social-ethical alternatives to the reality of Empire—a reality characterized by civilizational conflict, and by the complex system of a colonized lifeworld that is embedded within practices of greed, dominion, and ecological devastation. This series—Missional Church, Public Theology, World Christianity—invites scholars to promote alternative church practices for life-enhancing culture and for evangelization as telling the truth in the public sphere, especially in solidarity with those on the margins and in ecological stewardship for the lifeworld.

Contextual Theology for the Twenty-First Century

Edited by
Stephen B. Bevans
and
Katalina Tahaafe-Williams

PICKWICK *Publications* · Eugene, Oregon

CONTEXTUAL THEOLOGY FOR THE TWENTY-FIRST CENTURY

Missional Church, Public Theology, World Christianity 1

Pickwick Publications
An Imprint of Wipf and Stock Publishers
199 W. 8th Ave., Suite 3
Eugene, OR 97401

www.wipfandstock.com

ISBN 13: 978-1-60899-960-6

Cataloging-in-Publication data:

      Contextual theology for the twenty-first century / edited by Stephen B. Bevans and Katalina Tahaafe-Williams.

      xi + 140 p. ; 23 cm. —Includes bibliographical references

      Missional Church, Public Theology, World Christianity 1

      ISBN 13: 978-1-60899-960-6

      1. Christianity and culture. I. Bevans, Stephen B., 1944–. II. Tahaafe-Williams, Katalina. III. Title. IV. Series.

BR118 .C65 2011

Manufactured in the U.S.A.

Stephen Bevans dedicates this work to
Robert J. Schreiter,
Friend, Colleague, Mentor, who encouraged him
from the beginning

Katalina Tahaafe-Williams dedicates this work to
Sosaia Tu'uta Tahaafe,
her first ever teacher of contextual theology,
and to *Andrew* and *Lilliani,* who keep her sane

Contents

PART 3
Contextual Theology and the Mission of the Church

theory and practice must work hand-in-hand

learning how to live and act together

Preface

across different cultural backgrounds

THIS BOOK IS THE result of a conference on Contextual Theology held at United Theological College (UTC), Sydney, Australia, in April 2009. The conference was sponsored by Communitas,[1] the Contextual Mission and Theology Program of UTC. Communitas was tasked with the role of creating spaces for encounters that are transformative and life changing for people. Its brief was to offer opportunities for the diverse and rainbow people of God to find exciting and life-giving nourishment through the eyes, stories, experiences, and spirituality of "others," who would then return to their own communities and daily realities in dramatically new ways. The Communitas space is one where difference is not only valued but also welcomed and engaged with in mutual respect, compassion, and love. To paraphrase Sarah Mitchell, a former principal of the college, Communitas enables the people of God to join God's missiological adventure of *kingdom building* in the world, by learning with gusto how to live and act together across the many different cultural backgrounds that are God's gift in creation.[2] A core theological concern of the Communitas program is rooted in the absolute conviction that theory and practice must walk hand in hand and that this is the only way to expose and experience theology at its very best.

So the theology and philosophy behind Communitas totally influenced and shaped the agenda, topic, inputs, and content of the conference,

1. The term is borrowed from the anthropologist Victor Turner in reference to a community in process, one that has crossed a threshold, entering an in-between time and space where the process of transformation—of becoming something new and creating new life—takes place. See Turner, *The Ritual Process*, vii. The program is under the directorship of Katalina Tahaafe-Williams, who was appointed to the post in December 2007.

2. Mitchell, "Communitas of Christ," 181.

which was titled "What Has Contextual Theology To Offer the Church of the Twenty-First Century?" The topic of the conference emerged out of the struggle to articulate some answers to concerns about how theology can be in dialogue with life as it is experienced and lived by twenty-first-century Christians who are very diverse themselves and who live in contexts that are extremely diverse and multicultural. The assumption made is that contextual theology is uniquely placed to provide some answers to these concerns, and the speakers were identified exactly because of their social and cultural locations, not to mention their vast contextual theological knowledge and experiences.

Further, for those of us who are in the business of educating, training, and equipping the people of God for mission and ministry in the multicultural world of the twenty-first century, no less than such a paradigm shift in the epistemology of theology is necessary if we are to be effective in that task. It is not too harsh or radical to observe that in many places in Europe, and in the Western Christian context generally, our theologizing continues to be rather pale and monochrome because theory is still too remote from practice. And even in the Global South, Christians struggle to develop understandings of and ways to communicate Christianity that is free of such Western influence and open to the riches of local contexts.

Surely a sign of good health, as opposed to a sickly pallor, is vibrant color and energy. The conference and this resulting publication are our attempts to articulate what we believe should be characteristic of theology for the colorful and vibrant twenty-first century!

Stephen B. Bevans
Katalina Tahaafe-Williams
December, 2010

Acknowledgments

A FIRST WORD OF THANKS must go to the administration and staff of United Theological College of Sturt University in Australia for its support of Communitas and the work that the center is able to do with the resources that these institutions provide. In particular we are grateful for their support of the conference from which this book emerged.

Secondly, we are grateful to the many women and men behind the scenes at the conference—those who worked the registration tables, those who managed the electronic equipment that was used, those who provided hospitality, those who contributed to the wonderful entertainment during the conference.

Third, we are very grateful to Wipf & Stock Publishers and Pickwick Publications for taking this project on and so carefully shepherding it through the editing and production process. We are particularly in debt to Christian Amonson, who first read and accepted our manuscript; then to copy editor Jacob Martin, and typesetter Ian Creeger.

Finally, we are grateful to the people with whom we share our lives. Katalina thanks her husband Andrew, and Steve thanks the members of the community he lives with: David Esterline, Tim Lenchak, Gary Riebe-Estrella, and Mark Schramm.

PART 1

Contextual Theology and the Twenty-First-Century Church

1

What Has Contextual Theology to Offer the Church of the Twenty-First Century?

Stephen B. Bevans

INTRODUCTION

*W*HAT HAS CONTEXTUAL THEOLOGY to offer to the church of the *twenty-first century?* This is the question that we will grapple with and hopefully come to some kind of answer to during the four days of this conference, and this is the question that I will attempt to answer partly in this opening keynote address.

In order to do this—albeit partially—I'm going to proceed in three steps. First, I'm going to try to answer the question, what is the church of the twenty-first century? Second, I'm going to try to answer the question, what is contextual theology? With the answers to these first two questions—ironically, questions of *context*—I think we will be in a position to answer the third and original question, what has contextual theology to offer the church of the twenty-first century?

WHAT IS THE CHURCH OF THE TWENTY-FIRST CENTURY?

A Church of Great Diversity

The first and most important thing one can say about our church today is that it is impossible to say much in general about it. It is incredibly diverse, and if we can speak about its mark of catholicity, we have to speak about its unity-in-diversity rather than its universality. I'm going to set out a number of characteristics of the church in the twenty-first century in this section, but not everything I say fits every church, and possibly nothing I say will describe one or the other church. This is already a clue to what a theology that is authentically contextual can contribute to the church today—or to churches, because each one has its own context.

A World Church

We can say, however, that our church of the twenty-first century has definitely become a global church, a world church, with the vast majority of Christians from the so-called Two-Thirds World. This is something, thanks to scholars like Andrew Walls and Lamin Sanneh, that we have known for some time, but let's quickly review the facts using David Barrett, Todd Johnson, and Peter F. Crossing's statistics published in the January 2009 issue of the *International Bulletin of Missionary Research* and the World Christian Database online.[1]

Just about a century ago, in 1900, there were 521,712,000 Christians in the world. In mid-2009, say Barrett, Johnson, and Crossing, there are 2,149,761,000. At the present rate of growth, which is 1.35 percent per year, there will be almost 2.6 billion Christians fifteen years hence, in 2025. The growth of Christianity is across the board, but where the growth has been most astounding is in the Two-Thirds World. While the growth of Christians in Europe and North America has averaged .12 percent and .66 percent respectively per year since 1800, Africa has grown by a yearly rate of 2.59 percent, Asia—even with its minority of Christians—has grown 2.48 percent annually, Latin America has grown 1.17 percent, and Oceania has grown by 1.10 percent every year. The continent of Europe still has the largest number of Christians—about 531 million, projected to reach 539 million by 2025—and North America has about 221 million, with a projection of about twenty million more in fifteen years. However, Africa in mid-2009 had a Christian population of 447 million, projected to reach 662 million in 2025. Asia is at 366 million and will be at 490 million. Latin America has a population of 531 million, projected by 2025 to reach 623 million, and Oceania now has twenty-three million Christians

1. Barrett, et al., "Christian World Communions," 32; Barrett, et al., World Christian Database.

and will have twenty-six million in a decade-and-a-half. In 1900 the largest Catholic country in the world was France. In 2009 the first three largest Catholic countries are Brazil, Mexico, and the Philippines. As Andrew Walls concludes, "Christianity began the twentieth century as a Western religion, and indeed *the* Western religion; it ended the century as a non-Western religion, on track to become progressively more so."[2]

For Many Churches, a Minority Church

In Africa, and the church in Latin America and perhaps Oceania, Christians will make up the majority of the population. In Asia, Europe, North America, New Zealand, and Australia, however, Christians are now and will continue to be in the minority. According to the World Christian Database, Botswana has a population of 1.8 million and has 1.6 million Christians. Other African countries would have a similar ratio of Christians, even though others—like Burkina Faso—might have only a Christian population of about 50 percent. Latin American Countries would be similar to Botswana.

China however, with 1.2 billion people, has only about one hundred million Christians by a generous count. India's population of one billion contains about fifty-two million Christians, and Indonesia's twenty-seven million Christians make up less than 10 percent of the country's 226 million people[3]—even though these are more Christians than the entire population of Australia.

We all know from personal experience how the Christian population of Europe, Australia, and New Zealand is diminishing. My country of the United States is still quite religious, but it, too, is going the way of Europe and your countries.

What this means for the church of our twenty-first century is that many of us exist in a kind of diaspora situation. For some churches, like those of Indonesia and India, for example, it means living, worshipping, and doing mission in the context of an overwhelming non-Christian population. For others, like China and Vietnam, it means being Christian in a situation of suspicion and even persecution, subtle or not so subtle. Still other Christians, like those here in Australia and those in North America, will live out our Christianity in a state that is more and more secular and

2. Walls, "From Christendom to World Christianity," 64.

3 World Christian Database.

a society that is more and more multicultural and multireligious—which is our next point.

For the Churches of the One-Third World, a Multicultural Church in a Multireligious Population

We live in a world today of significant shifts in population. Since about the mid-1960s we have seen major movements of migration from Africa, Asia, Oceania, and Latin America to the wealthier parts of the world that a century ago were the colonizers of these areas. There is significant migration from Africa to Europe and North America; from Asia and Oceania to Australia, New Zealand, North America, and Europe; and from Latin America to North America. The migrant populations today are not like those of the past, whose goal was to assimilate themselves into the receiving culture. Rather, there is a strong effort to maintain cultural and religious identity. Our churches reflect the richness and the difficulties of these situations, and profiting from this multiculturality is a major challenge.

At the same time, there is and will continue to be a kind of assimilation of the various cultures. However, this assimilation seems more and more to be not so much an assimilation into the dominant culture as an assimilation into a totally *new* culture, one resulting from the blending of many diverse cultures in today's world. Soon after the election of Barack Obama, I saw a video essay on public television about an art exhibit at an American university. The exhibit consisted of a collection of portraits of young women and men who were of mixed race, like the newly elected president, and next to each face was listed the combination of races and cultures that contributed to each person's identity: one young man described himself, for example, as Filipino, Kenyan, White, and Chilean, while a young woman described herself as African-American, Samoan, and British. Next to his picture, another young man wrote, "I am the face of the future." This is a future that is not far away; in fact, it is with us now in our churches as we try to live the gospel in our twenty-first century.

A Young Church

Once again, this description might not fit all the churches of the world—however, it does fit the churches of Asia, Africa, Latin America, and Oceania, as well as the large numbers of people from these churches who have migrated to the churches of Australia, New Zealand, Europe, and North America. According to the World's Youth 2006 Data Sheet, posted by the Population Reference Bureau in Washington, DC, by 2025 only 17 percent of the population in affluent countries (e.g., Australia, United States, France, Japan) will be under twenty-four years old (in 2005 it was 19 percent). In contrast, in countries with the least affluent populations, around 27 percent of the population will be twenty-four or younger.[4] One would think that these statistics would obtain, as well, among peoples who have migrated to more affluent countries. Our church of the twenty-first century, especially where the church is flourishing, will be young, with more than one in four under twenty-four years old. Our churches will have to work at reaching and keeping the young.

A Persecuted Church

The church in the Minority World of the Global North is and is increasingly becoming a marginalized church. In many parts of the world, however, the church is a persecuted minority. In the last years we have heard about church bombings in Pakistan and Iraq, and the murders of missionaries and local Christians in India. In Latin America we hear of church leaders and church members being murdered for their stands on social justice. Several countries, like Indonesia, have laws that forbid citizens from converting to Christianity, and some states in Nigeria have decided that Muslim *Sharia* law is the law of the land. Barrett, Johnson, and Crossing perhaps exaggerate, but they estimate that there have been 17,600 Christian martyrs in 2009 alone. For a good number of our churches today, being a Christian means taking a risk, being under persecution.

A Poor Church

In the past, the majority of Christians lived in the most affluent part of the world. Now the majority of Christians live in the poorest part of the world: the church of the twenty-first century is and will continue to be a poor church. This is particularly the case since, with the decreasing numbers of church members in the One-Third World, there will be fewer and fewer funds available to share with other, less affluent churches. One example of this is my own Catholic missionary congregation, the Society

4 See http://www.prb.org/pdf06/WorldsYouth2006DataSheet.pdf.

of the Divine Word. In the past, our generalate in Rome was able to distribute tens of thousands, even hundreds of thousands of dollars for the work of our congregation in Papua New Guinea, Mexico, the Philippines, Ghana, and elsewhere. In the last several years this "annual distribution" has simply not been able to do what it had done in the past. The money is simply not there.

One implication of this situation for theological and church leadership is that there will be less funding for women and men from the Two-Thirds World to travel to more affluent countries for their theological and graduate education. Theological education will be more homegrown, more local, or students will be sent to other parts of the Two-Thirds World. In our religious congregation we already see this: many of our young confreres from India, Indonesia, and China are being sent to the Philippines to be educated rather than to Rome, Europe, or the United States, and Filipinos, too, are staying at home for their education. This may not guarantee a more contextual theological education, but the possibilities are there.

This new situation of the twenty-first-century church certainly causes difficulties, but it may also be a blessing. It will perhaps ensure that local churches live more simply and identify more with the situation of the people they serve. Perhaps for the first time since before the Constantinian era, the church of the twenty-first century is in a position to be a poor church—for the poor, with the poor, and of the poor.

This is a thumbnail sketch of the church of the twenty-first century. There may be other aspects that I have not treated (e.g., the church in the midst of drastic climate change), but I believe that what we have sketched here gives us a pretty good picture of the church to which contextual theology might have something to offer. It is an overwhelmingly Majority World church, one that is concerned with local cultures and social locations; one that is richly multicultural and lives in a multireligious world; one that is very young; and one that is a minority and often persecuted. In the One-Third World, the church is marginal to society and composed of many cultures and traditions. In sum, our church in the twenty-first century is a far cry from the church of a century ago, or perhaps even half a century ago. Ours is a church, as we will suggest, that needs a theology that is thoroughly contextual on the one hand and global or *intercultural* on the other.

WHAT IS CONTEXTUAL THEOLOGY?

As I have described or defined contextual theology in the second edition of *Models of Contextual Theology,*[5] contextual theology is a way of doing theology that takes into account (or we could say puts in a mutually critical dialogue) two realities. The first of these is the *experience of the past*, recorded in Scripture and preserved and defended in the church's tradition. The second is the *experience of the present* or a particular *context*, which consists of one or more of *at least* four elements: personal or communal experience, "secular" or "religious" culture, social location, and social change.

Depending on a number of circumstances—one's understanding of God's Revelation, one's attitude toward human experience, one's understanding of the normativity of Scripture or tradition—one might choose to enter into the mutually critical dialogue between past and present according to one—or a combination—of the six models I attempt to sketch out in my book. Each one of these models, I believe, is valid. There is not one model that is objectively better than the others. And yet the true validity of a model comes with its experience within a particular context. If the context is a homily that one has to give as a result of the recent Victoria bush fires, one might draw on the cherished values of courage and sacrifice that are found deep in the Australian psyche. Or, as a friend of mine told me who is a pastor in the town of Alexandra, which was in danger of being in the fires' path and near many of the burned areas, his congregation came together often and just kept silence, since there were no words to express their grief, although they did pray occasionally from the Book of Lamentations. If one is leading a discussion of white, middle-class Australian youth, one might reflect on how counter-cultural the message of Jesus could be in this affluent society today. Or, finally, if you are trying to give examples from a context that is not your own—like I have done in the three previous examples—you make an attempt to *translate* your experience and faith into examples and language that the people in that context might understand.

The key thing, though, as I have come to understand contextual theology and have reflected on it through the years, is the centrality of *experience*. It is the honoring or testing or critiquing of experience that makes theology *contextual*. What this means is that, for contextual theo-

---

5. Bevans, *Models of Contextual Theology* (2002).

logians, *anything* can be a source of theology: an experience of a sunrise in the Central Australian desert; a particular film, such as the critically acclaimed *Samson and Delilah*; a national event of tragedy (the bush fires) or wonder (Kevin Rudd's apology to Aboriginals); values in one's own culture; one's experience as a male or female; one's experience as a marginal person in one's culture; one's encounter with another religion; the experience of multicultural tensions in one's society; or the challenge of technology today.

When we recognize that Scripture and tradition are *records* of experience—the experience of liberation from oppressor Egypt, or of deliverance from starvation in the desert, or of the disappointment with kings, or of the encounter with Jesus of Nazareth, or of Paul's struggles to persuade communities not to insist on Jewish traditions, or of Arius' insistence on Jesus' creaturehood, or of a controversy over eucharistic presence or justification—we will recognize that doing contextual theology is doing exactly what the authors of Scripture and the makers of tradition did. While there is no question of the normativity of these sources of theology, we have to realize that when *they* were doing the theology that resulted in a particular book of Scripture or a particular doctrinal expression, the only thing they had was their present experience in their particular context and the norming texts, doctrines, personages, and art of their past. In that way, we are just like them—like the compiler of the prophecies of Isaiah, like Paul, like Athanasius, like Hidegard, like Luther or Wesley, like Mary McKillop or Dorothy Day. This is why I strongly believe that even though Scripture and tradition are our great sources for theology as well as for norms for theology's fidelity to the gospel, our present experience, our context, needs to be regarded as equal to them both. Our experience today—of reconciliation between the Aboriginal People and Australians, of the fear of terrorism and the need for interreligious dialogue, of our being marginalized within the context of secular culture—can and will be the tradition of tomorrow.

For me, then, contextual theology is a theology of rich and challenging dialogue: dialogue that tries to articulate my context, my experience, and dialogue of this experience with the experience of Christians down through the ages that we find in Scripture and Christian tradition.

movie
song

Dialogue

WHAT HAS CONTEXTUAL THEOLOGY TO OFFER THE CHURCH OF THE TWENTY-FIRST CENTURY?

I hope that, as we have sketched out the shape of our church today and of the future, and as we have reviewed our understanding of contextual theologizing, it has become clearer what contextual theology has to offer to today's church. A theology that honors the experience of context will be one that is not tied to Western ways, themes, and methods of theology. This may be very good for the West, but for the churches of Africa, Asia, Latin America, Oceania, and the churches of particular ethnic groups within the churches of the West (Aboriginal, Maori, African-American, etc.), theology should only be done from local experience and local context. The non-Western churches can also contribute to the global church by showing the church what it is: not a Western religion, but one that has been and is again a non-Western religion.

In churches that are in a minority status within secular or non-Christian minorities, their context might very well impel them to do theology—on the one hand—that emphasizes the uniqueness and difference of their Christian faith, and—on the other hand—that helps Christians "give an account of the hope that is within them" (1 Pet 3:15) in the face of indifference, opposition, or even persecution. This latter may not be unlike the early apologists in the church, and the experiences of Justin or Origen may well be important sources for their own efforts. Multicultural churches need to explore this unique, challenging experience. There needs to be a dialogue between and among cultures, ethnic identities, and social locations.

In many churches, not only must a theology be done that engages the young, but young people need to be trained and cultivated as theologians. One of the great contributions of contextual theology is its insistence that theology is not something confined to highly trained academics. Indeed, as I point out in my book on models of contextual theology, contextualization is too important to be left only to the theologians. Theology is the birthright of the entire church, and this includes the world's youth. The evening before I wrote these pages in late March 2009, one of my students at Yarra Theological Union shared in class how she attended a day of reflection for youth, and one of the young people, a seventeen-year-old, gave a stunning presentation on spirituality that absolutely blew her away.[6]

The poverty and vulnerability of the church is also an experience that might very well take the twenty-first century church back to its origins, when it was a struggling minority religion in the vast and powerful Roman and Persian Empires. A theology that is done out of poverty and vulnerability will be able to inspire and uphold the church, as it did in those formative times.

These are some of the contributions that a theology that takes experience seriously—a contextual theology—can make to our global, minority-status, multicultural, young, persecuted, and poor church of the twenty-first century. It takes these situations seriously and does theology out of them. I think, though, that we might be able to summarize what contextual theology has to offer our church today and tomorrow in four additional points. Contextual theology offers the church a new *agenda* for its theologizing; it offers it new *methods*; it offers it new *voices*; and it offers it a new *dialogue*. Let me speak briefly about each of these offerings.

A New Agenda

Contextual theology offers the church of the twenty-first century a new agenda. The church of the New Testament did not have the same agenda as the post-Constantinian church, the third-century East Syrian Church, the medieval church, the Reformation church, or the sixteenth-century Chinese Church. The church of the New Testament, for example, did not have a proper *Christological* agenda, as it emerged as the church had to think through its understanding of Jesus in the light of its encounter with Greek thought. The church of the fourth century did not have a proper *eucharistic* theology, as it emerged in northern Europe as the more symbolic worldview clashed with the more concrete worldview of the Germanic tribes. Context not only shapes the content and method of our theologizing. It also determines the questions we ask and highlights the things we see as important.

Up until our own time, with a more "universal theology" being studied in Basel and Brisbane, at Cambridge and at Trinity in Singapore, in Dunedin and Nairobi, there has been a basic shape to the theological enterprise. Catholics call these the basic theological tracts; Protestants call

---

6. The student's name is Denise Lyons.

them the basic loci: God and Trinity, creation anthropology, grace, sin, Christology, church, and eschatology. In today's global, minority-status, multicultural, vulnerable church, however, other issues may well emerge, and already have. A major issue that has emerged is ecology, and in many ways it has reshaped the theology of creation. Groups such as Aboriginals and Native Americans have emphasized the importance of a theological reflection on space and land. Asian theologians have proposed a theology of harmony. Latin Americans have insisted that no theology can be worthy of the name without the centrality of the experience of the poor and God's promise of liberation. Latino/a populations in the United States, and several other groups, have begun to theologize around the experience of migration. These issues certainly do interact with the more traditional topics such as Christology, grace, and so on. But they are new questions, and will develop not only new answers but also new ways of understanding the classic questions of God, of church, of creation, and of the end of the world. This is part of what contextual theology has to offer the twenty-first-century church.

new questions

A New Method

Contextual theology offers the church of the twenty-first century a new method. My book *Models of Contextual Theology* gives an overview of some of the new ways that a theology that takes experience seriously can proceed: more cautiously by a method of translating traditional formulations into particular languages, cultures, situations; taking more risk by trusting the context to guide new ways of thinking about the faith; letting action take the lead to forge new or deeper understandings of God's transforming grace in the world; and trusting the gospel story to challenge and critique an experience or a context. Other theologians, either in response to my book or independently, have proposed other models and methods. Theologians such as James and Evelyn Whitehead, Don Browning, Thomas Groome, and Neil Darragh have proposed models of practical theology that also propose, in various ways, a dialogue between tradition and context for transformative action. The Lumko Institute in Johannesburg, South Africa, has proposed a method of Bible sharing that helps people read the Bible out of their daily experience.

particular languages, cultures situations,
action
a dialogue between tradition + context for transformative action

But contextual theology has also opened up the notion of theology as something wider than mere verbal discourse. It can be the works or interpretations of local artists: poets, novelists, playwrights, painters, and sculptors. It can be the skilled use of proverbs. It can be the doing of or reflecting upon dance, or liturgy, or music. Last year at our annual meeting of the American Society of Missiology, I was enthralled by a presentation on the theology in the hymnody of the people of a very small tribe in (I believe) the Republic of Cameroon. Recently, I have been touched in a way that no discursive Christology could do by the "Jesus Laughing" exhibit on the Internet sponsored by Australia's Major Issues and Theology Foundation, Inc. (MIAT). During this past Holy Week I was awed by the paintings on the church walls of Santa Teresa, a small Aboriginal town south of Alice Springs. The paintings were done by a number of local Aboriginal women—none of whom had any special training in theology or art. Contextual theology can offer the twenty-first-century church new and creative methods for probing experience in the light of faith.

New Voices

There have been strong, clear, and beautiful voices in the past: Perpetua, Bardaisan, Alopen, Aquinas, Luther, Sor Juana, Barth, Dorothy Day. Theology that comes out of a world church, a minority church, a multi-cultural church, a poor church can open our ears to new voices—some right in our own back gardens, as it were, and others from contexts very different than our own. Several months ago, on a visit to the Philippines, my friend José de Mesa introduced me to a former doctoral student of his, Estela Padilla. As we talked I realized that she was one of the freshest voices in theology that I had heard for a long time. Her new voice needs to be listened to in the Philippines, and in other churches of our twenty-first century. My own US church needs to listen to older voices like Roberto Goizueta, Orlando Espín, Diana Hayes, and Peter Phan, and to younger voices like Miguel Díaz, Nancy Pineda Madrid, Vanessa White, and Jonathan Tan. The Australian Church needs to listen to its indigenous theologians, its young theologians from the Pacific and from Asia.

I could go on naming names, but I think my point is clear: The voices of contextual theologians are one more gift that contextual theology has to offer the church of the twenty-first century.

A New Dialogue

Lately, I have encountered a real problem with doing contextual theology, and this problem prompts me to suggest that we can take the doing of contextual theology one step forward. The problem with contextual theology, as I express it often these days, is that it is *contextual*. What I mean by this is that contextual theology can be so rooted in its own context that it can no longer communicate or talk with the theology of other peoples or other churches. I mentioned above that I have recently met Filipina theologian Estela Padilla and thought hers was one of the freshest voices in theology that I have ever heard. The problem, though, is that only Filipinos can read Estela's work, because she insists in writing in Tagalog. Any other language, she says, could not capture the full reality of what she wants to say. However, my sense is that Estela's work must get to other people around the globe. Her thought will not be fully translatable, of course, but I think that she can enrich and challenge other contextual theologians to do some of the creative thinking that she has done. And, I believe, responses to her could deepen her own efforts at developing a theology of the body, and a theology of ministry out of that theology, in Philippine context. What I propose, therefore, is that we need a wider dialogue among contextual theologians. Besides specific, focused contextual theologies, we need a theology that is done out of the dialogue *among* contextual theologies: a theology in global perspective.

The reason for this is that besides *our own* particular contexts, there is another context for doing theology in the church of the twenty-first century, and that is the global context. I think that integral to the development of our own contextual theologies is the need to enter into conversation with other contextual theologians and theologies. The dialogue will deepen our own insights, perhaps, as we see similarities between our own theology and that of a very different culture or social location. Or perhaps our understandings will be challenged by the insights that another context can provide. Or perhaps in the conversation both contextual theologies will be stretched and enriched. I have begun to speak of the need to read other theologies *analogously*—to realize that there might be a similarity-in-difference between the theology of my own context and that of others—one that can enlighten, stretch, challenge, and inspire my own efforts. My Filipino friend José de Mesa speaks of the need for *intraditionality* in theology, whereby one comes to a deeper understanding and articulation of one's own tradition in a conversation with other traditions. As I say, I see this as a next step for contextual theology. It is one that still honors one's own context and experience, while seeking a dialogue with others for the sake of that contextual understanding, and for the sake of the wider context in which we all live: our global church of the twenty-first century.

This is where my own work has taken me in the last several years. I have just finished writing a book titled *Introduction to Theology in Global Perspective*. It will be published by Orbis Books later this year and is part of the series of theology in global perspective edited by the Vietnamese-American theologian Peter C. Phan.[7] The book is an attempt to introduce students to doing theology—a theology that is always contextual—but it draws on the wisdom of many theological voices from many different parts of the world. It is, as I describe it, a "baby step" in the direction of a global theology, but I think it is one in the right direction. I've tried as well to take this approach in courses that I teach on the Trinity and on the church. I've published a reflection on the Trinity course in the Summer 2008 issue of the journal *Theological Education*.[8]

CONCLUSION

We are at a new crossroads in the history of the church, one that is perhaps as important as the decision, recorded in Acts 15, not to burden Gentile believers with Jewish customs; perhaps as important as when Constantine declared the rapidly growing Christian church a legal religion in his empire; perhaps as important as when Luther nailed his ninety-five theses on the church door at Wittenberg; perhaps as important as Europe's encounter with Americans, Asians, and Africans at the end of the fifteenth century. Contextual theology can help us deepen our appreciation of God's gift of our senses, our cultures, our genders, and the circumstances of our lives. It can offer the church, perhaps for the first time in its history, the gift of its own multi-splendored identity, a new appreciation of its unity and catholicity, its amazing holiness and its being rooted in those who knew the Lord in his earthly ministry. What has contextual theology to

---

7. The book was published in September 2009.

8. Bevans, "DB 4100."

offer the church of the twenty-first century? In a word, I think, it offers the church a new look at *itself*.

2

The Centrality of Contextual Theology for Christian Existence Today[1]

James Haire

INTRODUCTION

CONTEXTUAL THEOLOGY IS INCREASINGLY central for Christian existence throughout the world. It is central because Christianity is growing in the Global South, that is, in the world of contextual theologies, or *theologiae in loco* as they were first called. It is central because these contextual theologies of the Global South are lived out in communities' lives but not always recognized for what they are. It is central because often in the Global North, and in the Global South, too, these contextual theologies are regarded as of little significance for Christian existence throughout the world, including in their own places. Asia has been at the very heart of the history of contextual theology. Indigenous Asian

1. Parts of this paper were delivered at the joint Australian Association of Mission Studies (AAMS) and Charles Sturt University (ACC&C and PACT) Conference on "The Christian Message in the Public Square" in Canberra, Australia, in October 2008, and published in the *CTC Bulletin* 24:3 (which grants permission to publish them here). Some of the ideas in this paper were also introduced at the World Council of Churches (WCC)/Christian Conference of Asia (CCA) Consultation on "Towards Revitalizing the Ecumenical Movement in Asia" in Dhaka, Bangladesh, in September 2008. This paper has been peer reviewed, and fulfils the criteria for original research as set out by the Australian Government Department of Innovation, Industry, Science, and Research (DIISR).

Christian theology has, of course, a very long history, as outlined so clearly by Samuel Moffett,[2] and then by Gillman and Klimkeit.[3] However, we can see the development of self-conscious *theologiae in loco* and then contextual theologies in Asia since the late 1950s. A vast literature has been produced on the issue of intercultural theology since the first discussions of the so-called *theologiae in loco* took place in the late 1950s, now sixty years ago. The Asian movement for contextual theologies, like other such movements around the world, was very aware that the authentic gospel[4] or Christ-Event-for-us is not prepackaged by cultural particularity, but is living. The church always remains in a constant struggle between the acceptance of the Christ Event within its particular culture in each place, and yet the wrestling with that which stands over against its own particular acceptance in each place. In this sense the church is always both indigenous and *reformata sed semper reformanda* (reformed but always to be reformed). If the Christ-Event-for us in each place lives in widely diverse cultures, then for the whole people of God throughout the whole world there can only be a true fullness of that Event or that gospel if there is true interconfessional, intertraditional, international, interracial, and intercultural fellowship. The church of Jesus Christ, indeed, is a fellowship that transcends space and time. The gospel, especially today, can only be lived in its fullness through sustained and widespread intercultural theological reflection and *praxis*. This fact is important for Christians throughout the world, and especially for Christians in Asia. It is important for Christians throughout the world to take indigenous theologies seriously, not just as marginal or decorative, in that central truths of the faith are often being expressed in them with greater clarity than elsewhere. It is important for Asian Christians to press the insights of contextual theologies as pivotal for international Christian self-understanding in dogmatics, apologetics, missiology, and interfaith discourse.

In this chapter I wish to do a number of things. I wish to look at a very significant complex of indigenous Asian theological thought and *praxis*. To do that in an authentic way, I need first to look in some detail at this specific Asian culture and worldview. Second, I need to look at some

2. Moffett, *A History of Christianity in Asia*.

3. Gillman and Klimkeit, *Christians in Asia before 1500*.

4. Throughout this essay, "the Gospel" is used in the Bultmannian sense of "the Christ Event" or "the Christ-Event-for-us" or "the Christ-Event-for-them," etc. "The Christian message" or "gospels" are used for the written and oral traditions.

of the interactions between the preliterary world from which this culture comes and the Islam and Christianity that entered its world. Third, I need to examine this significant indigenous Christian theology in its context. From this, we will then be able to see how a contextual indigenous Christian theology provides not only for Christian dogmatics and apologetics but also for missiology and interfaith dialogue around the world. In this perspective, such a contextual theology has a vital place in international Christian existence in our time. Contextual theology must not, therefore, be seen as marginal or decorative, but as central to the international theological struggles of the church throughout the world.

There is a French proverb, which may have come from French experience throughout the world, which runs, "Il n'y a que les details qui comptent" (Only the details are really important). Mircea Eliade found it very illuminating in relation to cultures.[5] Certainly, it fits in with this study. Our "way in" on this occasion is not to be via a study on the history of religions, nor via a dialogue with non-Christian living faiths, nor via a phenomenological analysis of religious appearances, although naturally all of these will impinge upon the work.

I wish on this occasion to look at that all-embracing facet of human, and in particular religious, life for which we use the code words "animism," "primal religions," or "preliterary religions." No term that I know of is totally appropriate in this field,[6] and that is the experience of many researchers in the area of cultural[7] interchange, and in particular in the area of interaction between the gospel and cultures. I wish on this occasion to use the term *preliterary* in relation to these life-systems and worldviews, including the religions, in a purely descriptive way. No value judgement is applied to it. It has its disadvantages; however, other terms have as great, if not greater, difficulties.

---

5. Eliade, *The Quest,* 37.

6. The term *preliterary* is used to stress the fact that these religions have a long-developed tradition the origins of which would appear to predate the appearance of literary forms in the various religions. The term, therefore, seems more neutral and purely descriptive in its use than many other terms (e.g., animistic, primal, primitive). Other terms (e.g., tribal, customary, traditional) seem possible, but also appear to be more applicable to other religions as well than the present use of *preliterary*.

7. Throughout this essay, *culture* and *cultural* denote the total life pattern of social life including religion, rather than the artistic as distinct from other activities, such as those of politics, trade, or religion. The term is thus used as it is used by social anthropologists rather than as it is used by historians of the arts.

In the sense outlined above, preliterary life-systems and worldviews underlie all religious expressions in Asia, and not only in Asia, of course. On this occasion I wish to take one Asian preliterary system in which I have been involved in research for some considerable time. I wish to look at a number of aspects of it in some detail, and also to make some comparisons with aspects of other preliterary systems. I wish to look at it carefully, as this provides the basis for a strong and sustained understanding of the Indigenous Christian contextual theology. Moreover, I wish to look at the interaction of these preliterary forms and certain aspects of other religions, in particular Islam and Christianity.

In doing so I wish to bear in mind such questions as: What is the God whom we as Christians know *en prosopo Iesou Christou* (in the face of Jesus Christ [2 Cor 4:6]) saying to us in these preliterary forms? And what is God saying to us in these interactions?

INDIGENOUS BELIEF AND PRAXIS

The area in which I have been involved in research is the group of North Moluccan Islands in Eastern Indonesia. From an anthropological viewpoint, it is an extremely useful area in which to carry out research, for a number of reasons. First, a comparison of historical accounts by travelers over the past four centuries[8] indicates only the very slightest changes to indigenous preliterary forms over that period. This is very different from the situations, for example, in some South Pacific Islands[9] or among the varied Australian Aboriginal groupings,[10] where Asian or European influences have so altered preliterary forms that today we cannot really know what they were even two centuries ago. As a result it is very difficult to comprehend how the whole system works, or even which are the genuine vestiges of any original system.[11] Second, population change through immigration has been very limited.[12] Third, the heartlands of the preliterary

---

8. E.g., Baretta, "Halmahera en Morotai," 116ff.; Campen, "De Godsdienstbegrippen," 438–41, especially 438–39; Campen, "De Alfoeren," 284–97, especially 293.

9. Garret, *To Live Among the Stars*, passim.

10. Turner, "Tradition and Transformation," 189, 192–93.

11. Turner, "Terra Incognita," 18.

12. The only significant movement of population was that of the Sangihe and Talaud Islanders into the area.

systems have been very isolated; an almost "laboratory-type" situation has occurred.

In looking at this preliterary system, and in comparing it to others, we shall be mainly concerned to look at the beliefs, and the interaction of beliefs, from the standpoint of the believers, that is, of those involved in the life-systems. We shall not, therefore, be primarily concerned to discuss the various beliefs in terms of structural-functionalism or any other socioanthropological models.[13]

In other words, we are vicariously involved in "being there" in all senses, as far as that is possible, of course. To the North Moluccan, of course, could be applied the words of Williamson concerning the Akan of Ghana, that "the integration of his religious views and practices lies not in the fashioning of theological and philosophical structures, but in his socially inculcated personal attitude to the living universe of which he is a part."[14] It is, of course, impossible from a Northern Moluccan point of view to dissociate in any way so-called religious beliefs from a total understanding of life and the world.[15] For theological reasons, however, we have chosen that particular part or aspect of the totality of life that is the particular focus of the meeting of the Christian message with other beliefs as our departure point in this investigation. In doing so, however, we must attempt to be true to the North Moluccan viewpoint in not extrapolating one particular part of the whole but rather in using one particular "way in" to view the whole.

In the North Moluccas, the term *gikiri* was and is used as a generic word for one of the many local or personal divinities. However, it is clear that the word originally had a much wider meaning. Hueting in 1908 saw the basis of its meaning as "levend wezen, mensch, iemand"[16] (living being, spirit, human being, someone/anyone). In other words, he saw in it the elements of *mana*,[17] permeating nature in general and human beings in particular. Elsewhere, Hueting noted that "de mensch bestaat uit

---

13. I.e., we are not dealing with the issue primarily from such a standpoint. On this, see Rex, *Key Problems*, 175–90.

14. Williamson, *Akan Religion*, 86.

15. Thomas, "Penjebaran Agama," 19.

16. Hueting, *Tobèloreesch-Hollandsch Woordenboek*, 100.

17. See Hadiwijono, *Religi Suku Murbu di Indonesia*, 11, 17.

roehe,[18] gìkiri of njawa[19]en gurumini"[20] (humanity consists of body, gìkiri or njawa and gurumini). What is significant here is that it would seem there are two kinds of mana operative in North Moluccan religious understanding; for Kruijt has observed that, while gìkiri is found in human beings, animals, and plants, *gurumini* is found additionally in animals and especially in humankind.[21]

What seems clear is that among the Northern Moluccans, the gìkiri was originally a mana-type concept more connected with a Supreme Being,[22] while gurumini was originally a mana-type concept more related to the physical needs, particularly in relation to mobility, in creatures,[23] although in humanity the two were very closely connected.[24] However, it is the gìkiri that is "het onstoffelijke van den mensch, datgene wat ook na den dood voortleeft"[25] (the immaterial element of humanity, that which also lives on after death), in all cases.[26] Moreover, the gìkiri has a connection with plants and agricultural and forest areas that the gurumini has not.[27] It is for this reason that "spirit" or "god" seems a more appropriate translation than "soul," although no translation exactly covers the meaning-spectrum.[28] This mana-type concept is still seen today in that the power or the gìkiri is particularly seen in "objects, for example stones

18. I.e., Tobelorese for *body*.

19. *Njawa* is a Malay word which, as used in the North Moluccas, has a meaning very close to that of "gìkiri."

20. Hueting, "De Tobèloreezen ," 217–358, especially 251 and 137, n342.

21 Kruijt, "De Rijstmoeder in den Indischen archipel," 361–411.

22. Nothing specific is *here* implied about such a Supreme Being.

23. Despite his uncertainty as to how to translate this term (see Hueting, "De Tobèloreezen," 252–53), Hueting uses the word *levenskracht* (vital strength) for "gurumini."

24. Kruijt, 23, uses the term *zielestof* for both; he uses *zielestof* rather than *ziel* because the gìkiri and the gurumini are not in particular places (or in a particular place) in the body or plant but rather are diffused like a fluid or ether throughout it. (*Ziel* means "soul"; *zielestof* means "soul-material.")

25. Heuting, "Geschiedenis der Zending," 72 (1928) 1–24, 97–128, 193–214, 289–320; 73 (1929) 1–31, 97–126, 289–320; 74 (1930) 1–32, 97–128,193–234.

26. In limited cases; the gurumini also has a life after death.

27. Hueting, "De Tobeloreezen," (1922) 221–24. In the Northern Moluccas, plant life is closely connected with human and animal life; cf. Fox, "Sister's Child as Plant: Metaphors in an Idiom of Consanguinity," 219–52.

28. E.g., Hueting moves between *geest* (spirit) and *ziel* (soul) in translating gìkiri, but seems partially dissatisfied with both; see Hueting, *Tobèloreesch-Hollandsch Woordenboek*, 100; Hueting, "De Tobeloreezen," 25–252.

or tree-roots which have extraordinary forms" (in Indonesian, benda-benda, umpama batu, akarkaju jang bentuknja gandjil-gandjil).[29] It is also seen, however, in humanity.

It is doubtless from the breadth of the applications of the gikiri-concept that the term *Gikiri Moi* was related to the concept of a High God. We can see that, from gikiri, which we translate "spirit" or "god," and *moi*, the general North Moluccan word for "one," Gikiri Moi implies "the One God" or "the One Spirit." Thomas sums up the present understanding of Gikiri Moi as "'the One God' (or 'Lord'), who is head of all powers which are animistic, dynamistic or mana" (in Indonesian, Tuhan Jang Satu, jang mengepalai segla kekuatan-kekuatan jang animistis, dinamistis maupun mana).[30]

Hueting defined the term in a similar way, as "het oppperste wezen, de eerste der geesten (God?)"[31] (the supreme being, the first of the spirits [God?]).

However, it would seem to be inaccurate to think of Gikiri Moi in terms of a *deus otiosus*.[32] His connection with the life of the world is rather as "misschien *de* gikiri of de *voornaamste* gikiri"[33] (perhaps *the* gikiri or the *principal* gikiri). For this reason, Gikiri Moi is regarded as the Great God or Spirit in whom all the various gikiri have their unity and meaning; although each gikiri might appear to be more powerful than Gikiri Moi, this power is the power of immanence or presence; Gikiri Moi holds the unity in that the North Moluccans do not tend to distinguish between higher and lower powers but rather to experience each microcosm as the pertinent presence of the macrocosm at that time.[34]

It would seem that Gikiri Moi was the primary term associated with this Unifying God. However, other terms are found, too, the most common being *Djou Ma Datu* and *Djou Latala*. The word *Djou* is found in Tobelorese, Galelarese, and Ternatenese,[35] and means "Lord," and as

29. M. Rudjubik, "Kepercayaan Agama Kafir" [Heathen Beliefs], 3.

30. Thomas, "Penjebaran Agama Kristen," 20. *Tuhan* is the usual Indonesian for (the Christian) "Lord"; it is also frequently used for (the Christian) "God," in order to avoid using the standard Indonesian for "God" (including the Christian God), which is Allah.

31. Hueting, *Toboreesch-Hollandsch Woordenboek*, 100.

32. On this, see Tobing, *The Structure*, 21–23.

33. Hueting, "De Toboreezen," (1921) 258.

34. Cf. Tobing, *The Structure*, 21.

35. It is also a loanword in other North Moluccan languages.

such it was the primary title applied to the Sultan of Ternate,[36] who was formerly regarded as having the status of a demigod, too. It seems that the meaning of the term was then widened and applied to Gikiri Moi. However, in general it was used together with an epithet. *Ma Datu* (or *Madutu*) originally may have meant either "the true" (eigenlijke) or "the possessing" (eigenaar).[37] There is similarity, of course, between the two in that "the Lord who is the Possessing One" or "the Possessor" is for that reason "the true" or "real Lord." At the present time *Djou Ma Datu* is similar to Hueting's "de Opperheer, het Opperwezen, de eigenlijke Heer"[38] (the Sovereign, the Supreme Being, the true Lord) or "*de* heer"[39] (*the* Lord).

Latala is associated with another North Moluccan phrase, *Unanga Daku*, both of which imply "the One from above" or "the One above" (Hij daarboven).[40] However, it would seem that *Latala* or *Lahatala* is a localized form of the Malay/Indonesian expression for the Arabic-Muslim divine name, *Allah ta'ala*. Therefore, *Latala* (or *Lahafala*) is at source a loanword from Malay/Indonesian, and has replaced the North Moluccan *Unanga Daku*; it has been given the thrust of the meaning of *Unanga Daku* (above) because the Muslim God has been implied to be superior to the Highest Being (Gikiri Moi) in the preliterary belief. From this it would seem that originally perhaps Gikiri Moi was given the additional names of Djou, Djou Ma Datu, Unanga Daku, and Djou Latàla.

It would seem that there gradually came a tendency to pose a *deus otiosus* above Gikiri Moi—although, of course, related to him—and that such a God was associated with the names Djou Ma Datu and Djou Latala; he was the God who was the true and real Lord and the Possessor of all and the One Above All. Nevertheless, there was always a tension, with this dualism between Gikiri Moi and Djou Ma Datu/Djou Latala: on the one hand, Gikiri Moi was the very same as Djou Ma Datu/Djou Latala; on the other hand, he was no *deus otiosus*.

Below Gikiri Moi are the company of the *gomanga*, the spirits of the dead or, more accurately for the North Moluccans, the living-dead ("geest

---

36. On a similar use of "Kyrios" ("Lord"), see Arndt and Gingrich, eds., *A Greek-English Lexicon*, 460.

37 Hueting, "De Tobeloreezen," (1921) 258–59.

38. Hueting, *Tobeloreesch-Hollandsch Woordenboek*, 66.

39. Hueting, "De Tobeloreezen," (1921) 258.

40. Ibid., 259.

van afgestorvenen, zielen die men vereert")[41] (soul of the dead, spirits whom people revere). All gomanga are gikiri.[42] These living-dead involve a very considerable amount of the thinking of the North Moluccans. The basis of this concern with the gomanga is the uncertainty as to the future relationship between a North Moluccan tribesperson and a near relation of anyone of great influence in the village or tribe (in Indonesian, suku) who had died and so now lives in a new way.[43] The gomanga or living-dead can thus become a true friend, guardian, guide, and counsellor, or a very dangerous personal enemy. For this reason, the customs carried out at death must be done so with the utmost care. Campen reported in 1883 that on the death of the head of a household, it was customary to destroy most of his property, especially that of any value, so as to prevent his gomanga later having any regrets or jealousy over any possession that he could now no longer use;[44] in recent years, too, it has been known to occur. Funerary rites, then, involved the building of a small, separate *dooden huisje*[45] (house of the dead) beside a family's house, where the corpse was guarded for up to forty days; thereafter, sometimes the bones were buried, sometimes they remained in this small house, and some-times they (or some of them) were placed in the roof-space of the family's home.[46] In any case, the gomanga, after the due observation of these rites, was regarded as living with the family and the total village community; daily food would be placed in the roof-space as an offering to him.

These living-dead existed insofar as they had had influence in their previous life and had been given due funerary rites; and those people with the greatest influence in the past had the greatest "presence" or "existence" after death.[47] The gomanga as such were neutral in their attitude towards their families and community, as we have noted. However, a gomanga of great influence who was properly cared for both in his original funer-

---

41. Hueting, *Tobeloreesch-Hollandsch Woordenboek*, 109.

42. However, of course, not all gikiri are gomanga. North Moluccans say that the gomanga are "more refined than 'gikiri'" (in Indonesian, lebih halus dari 'gikiri'); by this it would seem that the gomanga are deemed higher than the other types of gikiri associated with birds, etc.

43. See Noss, *Man's Religions,* 21–24.

44. Campen, "De Alfoeren," 293.

45. Hueting, *Van zeeroover tot christen*, 12.

46. Hueting, "De Tobeloreezen," (1922) 154–157.

47. Rudjubik, "Kepercayaan Agama Kafir," 3.

ary rites and daily and annually thereafter could become the main guide, guardian, and hope of a person and their family. If, on the other hand, the rites were poorly observed both at death and thereafter, the gomanga could become a fearful enemy. However, one form of the gomanga from the outset was an implacable enemy. This was the gomanga *madorou*, who was one of the living-dead who was insulted at death by being given improper funerary rites.[48] He thus brought disaster at every opportunity, especially upon his immediate family.[49]

From what we have seen, it can be observed that in the preliterary religious understanding of the North Moluccans, the security-creating harmony most closely related to the Christian concept of salvation concerns protection from the village spirits, the correct relationship with other creatures and nature, the right ties with the gomanga, and the hoped-for respect that would guarantee one's future gomanga-status. It seems that for the North Moluccans in general it is accurate to follow Cooley's observations in the central Moluccas, that is, that "the indigenous religion and *adat* should be seen as two halves of a whole"[50] Although Gikiri Moi or Djou Ma Datu/Djou Latala has not given a specific law-code, nevertheless the gomanga and the village spirits provide the sanctions for the adat (customary law) system; and it is Gikiri Moi who sums up and holds together the various gomanga and other gikiri. For this reason the adat system has a close connection with the security-creating harmony that is dependant upon the relationship of a person with the gomanga and all the other gikiri.[51] This we can see in relation to that part of the adat that most concerned the population, that is, the issues of marriage and sexual relations. The correct actions in these matters, of course, were determined by what was correct within the tribe.[52] In the coastal regions of the North Moluccas, a man was quite free to have sexual relations with an "outside" unmarried girl.[53] However, an adulterous wife and her lover could be killed by the husband and his brothers. In fact, the effect of this outlook was to cause great stability in family life among the coastal peoples.

48. Cf. the Batak "hasangapon" in Pedersen, *Batak Blood and Protestant Soul*, 25.

49. Rudjubik, "Kepercayaan Agama Kafir," 4.

50. Cooley, "Altar and Throne," 482.

51. I.e., all the other gikiri including all the village-spirits.

52. I.e., in general, moral action only concerned those within the tribe.

53. I.e., with a girl from outside the village, and even more so with a girl from outside the tribe (suku). Even with a girl from within the village, penalties were not very severe.

This self-preserving intolerance to *howono* (the breaking of the adat) was presumably related to the fact that the coastal people were traditionally a seafaring people who had set up communities at great distances from their homeland; therefore, they needed a strict marriage adat in order to protect their stability.

On the other hand, in some interior agricultural plains, there was an annual fertility feast, known as *waleng*, the term referring to both the feast and the gikiri of fertility. The feast was held for seven to ten days at the end of harvest and before the new planting; during this time there was worship to the gikiri waleng, Gikiri Moi, and the gomanga, in addition to communal eating and merrymaking for a number of villages. Also, from dusk until dawn, there were communal sexual relations; during the period of the waleng, one did not concern oneself about who was one's wife or husband. The purpose of this was to give honor to gikiri waleng and to ask for fertility of the soil and of the produce in the coming planting season. Unlike the situation of the coastal, seafaring peoples, the significant difference of this interior adat was that it had in general very little sanction against adultery. Adultery in recent times, especially by the wife, was considered of little consequence. Thus, the attitude towards adultery and marriage-sanctity in Christian communities was very strongly influenced by the differing preliterary outlooks on the subject in coastal and inland areas. In coastal areas the wife's adultery was a very serious breaking of the adat, while in inland, agricultural areas it was considered to be of little consequence. This latter was, of course, related to the much greater significance of inland fertility cults.

So here we see an integrated system of preliterary belief and life.

CONTEXTUAL THEOLOGY IN WORD AND PRAXIS

It has seemed to me important to look in considerable detail at this pre-literary structure, so that we can appreciate the climate and outlook of such a system. Systems of this kind underlie many situations in Asia, and indeed in many parts of the world.

I now wish to look at the interaction between this system and the two world religions that came into the area, Islam and Christianity, both of which have very large formal followings. I wish to look at certain aspects of the mutual interactions of this preliterary system and Islam, and at some facets of the mutual interactions of this preliterary outlook and Christianity. I wish to pick up certain salient features, rather than give an overview, as I have done elsewhere.[54] Of course there were mutual interactions between Islam and Christianity, but that is outside the scope of this paper.

First, Muslim concepts influenced preliterary beliefs in a number of ways. There was clearly a strong Muslim influence on the development of the concept of Gikiri Moi as the One High God. This is confirmed in the application to God of the title Djou and the epithet Latala/Lahatala. However, while for Islam *Allah ta'ala* brought widely-diversified facets, the effect of this concept upon the concept of Gikiri Moi, without the fullness of the Muslim doctrine of God, was to make the latter somewhat of a *deus otiosus*. Again, the "clothing" of preliterary beliefs in Muslim nomenclature by the preliterary religionists themselves was to mean that not only were Muslim terms used but, more significantly, the Muslim dualism between good and evil was applied by the preliterary religionists themselves to *certain* living-dead and especially to the village spirits. Whereas before the relationship between that bringing good fortune or protecting and that bringing ill fortune was more complex, involving the varied relationship between a villager and the diverse living-dead and the various forms of the "aweful," the influence of Islam tended merely to posit the various evil spirits. There thus remained a tension between the older and the Muslim-influenced concepts of good and evil, or fortunate and unfortunate. Again, preliterary concepts influenced Islam as it developed in the region. For example, the preliterary outlook of the North Moluccans influenced Islam by encouraging the *Sufi* mystical movement in the area. It would seem that the preliterary animistic, dynamistic, and *mana* concepts encouraged the mystical and pantheistic tendencies of *Sufism* in the tradition of the ways of thinking originally associated with Ibn-al-Arabi of Murcia.

Second, preliterary influence on Christianity was and is considerable. A good example is the preliterary influence on *the understanding of the Triune God*, and on the relationship between the Triune God and the varied gikiri. There was an attempt to work out an integrated system between the Christian Triune God and the gikiri and village spirits. A tendency towards Sabellianism, of course, could be expected in that

54. Haire, *The Character*, 237ff.; cf. World Alliance of Reformed Churches Bali Consultation Report.

Gikiri Moi had been integrated into the greater Christian God, and this Christian God was the unifying basis of all the gikiri; and this in fact seems to have happened.[55] In this tendency to Sabellianism "à la North Moluccas" Christians regarded the various gikiri [56] as the microsmic presence in each place of one of the three facets of the Triune God, although the doctrine of the Holy Spirit tended to be greatly minimized. Unlike the situation in Ceram in the Central Moluccas, [57] in the North Moluccas the Christian God tended to be regarded more in terms of power-through-presence.

However, the second example, leading on from this first example, is more significant. It creates a significant indigenous *Christology*. As the gikiri, as we have seen, were related in general to the facets of the Triune God, so the gomanga were specifically related to the Sonship.[58] As we have seen, there were concepts of the Senior Living-Dead and the Unseen Leader. These preliterary outlooks were to have considerable influence on the Northern Moluccan Christian understanding of the relation between the divine and human in Christ. Thus, the North Moluccan Christians began to base their Christological understanding on the Senior-Living-Dead who was the Unseen Leader. They were the people (*bala*) who had been called out to follow the Lord Jesus as their leader. He could be related to them (that is, they could understand his humanity) because he had been alive but was now living after death in their villages, and as such was their Unseen Leader. That is to say, in the first instance he was quantitatively but not qualitatively different form their greatest ancestral gomanga. It is against this background that two New Testament themes were of great frequency in their preaching. First, the church and particularly the village congregation as the body of Christ were often used to stress the relationship of each humble villager's future gomanga with the

---

55. This tendency towards Sabellianism has, of course, often been inherent in Reformed thinking; cf. Barth, *Church Dogmatics I*, 403.

56. Here used in the generic sense, including the *gòmànga* and village spirits (the latter at least in part). When the gìkiri was potentially favorable or unfavorable, it was related to the Christian God. When it was entirely unfavorable, it was related to the power of evil.

57. Cooley, "Altar and Throne," 490; Haire, *The Character*, 256.

58. The Fatherhood of God was related to Gìkiri Moi as the unifying and meaning-giving basis of all the gìkiri, including the gòmànga.

gomanga (*the* gomanga) of Christ.[59] Second, Christ the forerunner and pioneer in Hebrews 12 was used, too, to relate the believer's gomanga to that of Christ.[60] We have seen that the preliterary influence of the *gamanga*-concepts tended to set no qualitative difference between Christ and believers, although there was a great quantitative difference. Set against this, however, and stressing the divine in Christ, was the "North Moluccan Sabellianism" which we have just seen, and which regarded Christ as the microcosmic presence in each congregation of the whole macrocosmic Christian God. This tended to result in an understanding of Christ that could fit in with the *vere deus, vere homo* of the Definition of Chalcedon of 451 CE. For the gomanga influence in North Moluccan thinking rendered a clear distinction between the divine and the human both impossible and incomprehensible in North Moluccan terms. They thought of Christ as the Great Gamanga. The gomanga-concept explained and integrated for the North Moluccans what was the Christological problem in Latin terms. On the one hand, as all the gomanga in preliterary terms found their meaning in Gikiri Moi, so Christ was the aspect of God most related to the lives of believers both before and after death. So he was truly divine (*vere deus*). On the other hand, as the Unseen Leader of all Christian gomanga,[61] He was the Head of the village congregational Body of the faithful. However, these two were not mutually opposed but could easily be mentally integrated. So, here we see a very significant new indigenous understanding of Christology.

It is against this background that we see the importance and significance of the North Moluccan *de facto* interaction with the Definition of Chalcedon. Chalcedon insists on three factors in relation to Christology. First, it insists that Christ is "truly divine." Second, it insists that Christ is "truly human." Third, it insists that Christ is one. Without doubt, this North Moluccan Christology sees Christ as truly human. As we have noted above, he could be related to them (that is, they could understand

---

59. I.e., based mainly on Rom 12:3–8; 1 Cor 12:12–30; Eph 1:22–23; or Col 1:18–20—the last reference, especially Col 1:18 where Christ is also called *prototokos en ton nekron* (the firstborn from the dead), being most supportive.

60. I.e., based particularly on Heb 12:1–17.

61. I.e., both the gomanga of the already living-dead and the anticipated gomanga of believers still alive. The Christian eschatological emphasis stimulated the application of gomanga, in the eschatological "already-but-not-yet" sense found in the New Testament, to still-living believers.

his humanity) because he had been alive but was now living after death in their villages, and as such was their Unseen Leader. That is to say, and as we have noted, he was quantitatively but not qualitatively different from their greatest ancestral gomanga. Again, without doubt, this North Moluccan Christology sees Christ as one. Moreover, it may very well see him as truly divine. Again, as we have noted above, there was great stress on the divine in Christ through the "North Moluccan Sabellianism," which, as we have seen, regarded Christ as the microcosmic presence in each congregation of the whole macrocosmic Christian God. Although there may be debate here, this North Moluccan Christology seeks to explain Christ, while Chalcedon is not able, in fact, to explain Him. Chalcedon rather only sets the *guidelines*, or *parameters*, as to what Christians are and are not to say about Christ in order to remain Christian. They must say that Christ is truly divine; they must say that Christ is truly human; and they must say that Christ is one. If they fail to acknowledge even any one of these fully, then they place themselves outside the fold of Christian believers. So Chalcedon is a marker, or a rulebook, rather than an explainer. The North Moluccan Christology has the following advantage over Chalcedon. In its own way, as we have seen, it is faithful to Chalcedon. It fully accepts the three emphases of Chalcedon. However, more than that, it *explains* Christology. It *explains* the Person of Christ in the North Moluccan context. It thus engages in dogmatics, but not simply dogmatics; it also engages in apologetics, and indeed takes part in the missiological task. Moreover, it provides Christian material for interreligious dialogue and discourse. It is of great value as Asian indigenous Christian theology. However, it is also of great value for international Christian understanding and dogmatics, for international Christian apologetics, for international Christian missiology, and for an international Christian contribution to interfaith discourse.

Following this, we come to another, very significant contribution to indigenous Asian Christian theology, this time in praxis. This third example indicates the preliterary influence upon the Christian understanding of *salvation*. We have seen how the preliterary concern for security-creating harmony, the concept most closely related to the Christian understanding of salvation, was based upon guarding the correct relationships in and around the village community, including the relationships with the *iikiri, gomonga*, the village spirits, other creatures, and nature in general. Implied in this also was a forward-looking concern for each person's gomanga-status after death. What seems to have happened with the advent of Christianity is that these concerns were baptized into North Moluccan Christian practice, while in addition an eschatologically oriented concept of salvation related to the grace and sovereignty of the Christian God was pursued. Moreover, there seems to have remained an unresolved tension between the two outlooks. On the one hand, the pre-literary salvation outlook had been primarily oriented to *the present* (the guarantee of the security-creating harmony), with the gomanga-status concern being an addendum to that. Both regarding the adat and illness and death, the thinking seemed to be that, as the gikiri sanctioned the adat and also had to be in correct harmony with the community for there to be security, and as through Gikiri Moi they had all been incorporated into the Christian God, so the correct observance of a Christian adat and the righting of wrongs through the church would guarantee security and harmony for the rest of the village

Running parallel with this outlook, on the other hand, was the *eschatologically oriented* understanding of salvation. Salvation in these latter terms seems to have been related to the fact that the Christian God was now ultimately responsible for the majority of the previous preliterary religionists, and so would be responsible in God's grace. However, there tended in this eschatologically oriented outlook to be less emphasis on salvation from sin. As sin was so closely connected with the breaking of the adat, so salvation from the consequences of sin was almost always related to the former, "baptized" preliterary security-and-harmony concept of salvation. Thus, under preliterary influence, a security-and-harmony-related understanding of salvation, primarily oriented to *the present* and largely baptized into Christianity, remained in unresolved tension with a more *eschatologically oriented* concept of salvation.

However, in one very clear manner, the two aspects of the North Moluccan understanding of salvation came together. This was in the issue of ecology and the integrity of creation. A very significant example of indigenous theological *praxis* gives a clear demonstration of this. In the 1980s, during the logging boom in the islands, a license was granted to an overseas company to log in an area of high-density timber of the highest international value and uniqueness. The concession set out terms for the logging; only one tree in ten was to be felled, and that tree was to be replaced through planting. The villagers, who were largely Christian of preliterary background, recognized that the terms of the license were not being carried out. Moreover, they saw great danger in any logging of this proposed scale taking place in any case. In fact, their overwhelming outlook was controlled by their concept of salvation, both present-orientated and eschatologically orientated, as we have seen above. They regarded the overseas logging company as merely irresponsible children, as endangering the integrity of creation and especially as being unfaithful to their concept of salvation. The villagers were humanly powerless but divinely empowered, in their own eyes. Thus, in darkness, day-by-day and week-by-week, they removed small parts of the logging machinery and hid them in the forest. The logging company brought in more and more equipment, with great trouble and at great expense. The villagers continued to remove and hide the small parts. The logging company was greatly frustrated, but could not work out how the parts of their equipment were disappearing. Finally, the logging company gave up, returned the license to the government, and left the area. No more logging took place. After this, the deeply pious villagers gave thanks to God for God's guidance and empowerment. They had absolutely no concept of carrying out sabotage, or of acting illegally. For them, it was clear simply that irresponsible outsiders, like irresponsible children, were engaging in activity that was, and would be, detrimental to both present-oriented salvation and eschatologically oriented salvation. Thus, from their indigenous North Moluccan theological prespective of salvation, they carried out a theological *praxis* of salvation.

We have thus seen the main formulations of indigenous Christian theology in thought and *praxis* among the North Moluccans. There were also others, which reinforced the contextual theology that we have observed.

As a fourth example, preliterary influence could also be seen in the understanding of the Sacrament of the Lord's Supper. If the Bible was the day-to-day contact point with God, so the Lord's Supper was the preeminent contact point where God through the Great Living-Dead Jesus Christ was supremely present. It was thus a truly "awful" occasion, potentially fraught with great danger but also capable of giving great blessing. In this understanding there were clearly influences from the high-feasts of Gikiri Moi and the gomanga. Fear was expressed in that any person attending the Lord's Supper with a hidden, unresolved sin was liable to face serious illness or death in the near future. It was also seen that the slightest flaw in the carrying out of the service could result in grave trouble for the community, as the Lord himself was in the process of holding his feast. Blessing, however, could be obtained both for each individual attending the Supper and especially for the whole community through the correct carrying out of the ordinance.[62]

A fifth example, closely related to this, was the preliterary influence upon the understanding and celebration of Christ's Passion. Thus, in the North Moluccas there was often a very close following of the details of Christ's suffering and death week-by-week and sometimes day-by-day up until the celebration of the Lord's Supper. Indeed, Christ was the great and senior gomanga, who was also the Hero (as Unseen Leader) who had undergone a violent death. Therefore the careful following and examination of the details of the passion, death, and resurrection of Christ could help guarantee His leadership and support of the congregation as His dependent *bala* (people) in the year ahead, and help protect them from the dangers always attendant upon their contact with such a great gomanga.[63]

A sixth example relates to Confirmation. A very strict procedure for the candidates was undergone at the hands of the church at the end of catechising, and if a potential communicant could show his or her spiritual strength in this then confirmation would ensue. Underlying this would seem to be the concept that through the catechetical process culminating in confirmation, the initiate's connection with the Great Gomanga (Christ) as Head of the Body, and through Him with God, was guaranteed.

Here, then, is an integrated complex of very significant indigenous Christian theological perceptions, of value not only to dogmatics but also to apologetics, missiology, and interfaith discourse.

INTERWEAVING, TRANSFIGURATION, AND DOUBLE-WRESTLE

As we consider the above analysis, we can observe three types of interaction. First, there is a tendency for preliterary views to be "baptized" *in toto* into Islam or Christianity. Second, there is the struggle between preliterary and Muslim viewpoints, on the one hand, and the struggle between preliterary and Christian outlooks, on the other. Third, there is the producing of new insights into Muslim, and particularly Christian, faith and

---

62. In North Moluccan thinking, material and spiritual (i.e., that related to the whole gikiri-complex) blessing could not be sharply differentiated from each other.

63. On this following of Christ's suffering, cf. *Heidelberg Catechism*, Question 79.

life. In relation to Christianity, this has produced contextual theologies of great significance internationally. Here, Asian Christian theology has an opportunity and responsibility in its international calling.

For Christianity, it is perhaps because the Christ Event can never be exclusively identified either with one culture or one type of culture that Paul employs the ambiguous term *he akoe* (the hearing) to describe the action by which the Christ Event enters a person's or a community's life, that is, the crucial step that leads to faith.[64] For, in a sense, in all the interactions described before and since H. Richard Niebuhr, that Christ Event must truly enter our world, and yet must also always be under the opposing divine criticism. This, in fact, is seen in the varied theologies in the New Testament.[65] It seems to me that a term such as *syncretism* has only limited value in relation to these issues, in that it tends not to look at the complex interactions such as we have noted above. Transition, translation, transposing, transplanting, transferring, transforming, and transfiguring are varying expressions of the intercultural activity to which Christians are called and in which theologians bear a special responsibility. In this, too, Asian theologians have an opportunity and a responsibility.

So, if we return to the issues at the beginning of this paper, we can see how the Christ Event must live, and yet transfigure, the culture in which it is placed, always at the same time struggling with the fact that it is the Divine that nevertheless has entered this world. There is a "double-wrestle." In the first five centuries of the church's life after the New Testament period, the outline within which dogmatic discussion was to take place was largely set. That involved the interweaving of the Christ Event into, and the transfiguration by the Christ Event of, Hellenism and its successors. However, if the Christ Event was also interwoven into, and transfigured, other cultures with rich backgrounds, as we have seen above, then could not its impact also bring further clarity in word and *praxis* in our time? If one looks at North Moluccan indigenous Christian theology, as an example of Asian contextual theologies, is not significant, new, and insightful clarity given there for dogmatics, for apologetics, for missiology, and for interfaith discourse around the world? Much of

---

64. See Taylor, *The Growth of the Church of Buganda*, 254. See, e.g., Rom 10:16–17; Gal 3:2.

65. See, for example, Käsemann, "Begründet der neutestamentliche Kanon die Einheit der Kirche?" and "Zum Thema der Nichtobjektivierbarkeit," (both subsequently published in Käsemann, *Exegetische Versuche*).

Western Europe and North America, and indeed Asia as a consequence, is heir to that Christ Event in Jewish, Greek, Latin, Celtic, Anglo-Saxon, German, and French traditions. However, are we forever to be controlled solely by the fact that the first post-Biblical God-talk took place in the Mediterranean basin? From what we have seen, it seems that contextual theology has a vital place in international Christian existence in our time. This is not to be seen in any triumphalist manner, but purely in the service of the church ecumenical. Contextual theology must not, therefore, be seen as marginal or decorative, but as central to the international theological struggles of the church throughout the world. In this, too, Asian theologians bear a special responsibility, calling, and opportunity.

3

The Cons of Contextuality . . . Kontextuality

Jione Havea

FAKATAPU

I BEGIN BY ACKNOWLEDGING—AS ANY respectful Tongan would do, following the customary practice of *fakatapu*, which is where one honors the *tapu* (taboo), the sacredness, of land and of people, in one's audience—that I am here sharing a reflection that I wrote, while being a migrant worker, in the country of the Darug people, in Australia. I am a foreigner to where I now live, so it is necessary to acknowledge and honor the tapu of my location, my context. I offer my fakatapu with the hope that I am permitted to think and reflect as a foreigner, a stranger, in a country that is intoxicated with the blood of Aborigines, First People, of many nations and communities, and of a multitude of settlers, Second People.[1]

Here, I must quickly add a caveat: Please note that my fakatapu is the first con of this contextualizing chapter! I write as a Tongan, but I am not currently located, physically, in Tonga. To be located, to be contextual, involves one being ideologically rooted and being creatively imaginative, but it seems that it is not necessary for one to be placed, actually, in order to be contextual. In the fakatapu that I have offered, therefore, I am like a

---

1. Budden, *Following Christ in Invaded Space*, 5–6; Brett, *Decolonizing God*, 8–12.

nationalist who does so from afar, or one who is patriotic from a distant land, as if I too believe that nationalism is possible without a nation. Can one be contextual without being rooted, actually, in the context of interest? What then does it mean to be contextual?

I acknowledged the country of the Darug people, but my respect is constructed with words, and I offer it neither in Tongan nor in the language of the Darug people. I appeal to one context in order to make me relevant in, permissible into, another context. In the interest of whom/what have I directed and located my takatāpu in the country of the Darug people and language? The answer is simple, and clear: it is in my interest. My con, in this case, is using the name of the Darug people in vain, and luring the sympathy of readers for the Aborigines of Australia, which has something to do with their/your own interests, in order to justify myself in my current context and permit me to engage you, the reader, in this reflection. I am the foreigner who sneaks myself into a new context, as if this, here, is my home.

Now, if you will, put in my place a contextual thinker, one who comes bearing a message or a way that she needs to contextualize. Doesn't she too come, and enact the process of contextualization—engaging us and our sympathies—in her own interests? What then is the place of context, from where she comes and into which she comes, both of which might be foreign to us, in her project? What makes her contextual? What makes her message or way contextual?

I do not pretend that contextualization is free of having blind spots. Reid-Salmon's lament that Black Theology omitted the Caribbean Diaspora experience is a telling exposure of one of the oversights of contextual thinking.[2] The same could also be said with regard to the omission of the experience of Black people, men and women, straight and LGBT, with their rich diversity, in South America and in Oceania, even in Europe and on islands. Whether any contextual statement can be inclusive enough, I am not sure. But the contextual raft must still be pushed forth.

inclusive

2. See Reid-Salmon, "A Sin of Black Theology."

DAMNED IF I DO, AND DAMNED IF I DON'T

Since this chapter began as an oral presentation for a conference on contextual theology, I will dance around the act of contextualization (or contextuality) with the hope to shake off some of the shackles with which contextual theologians yoke their hearts and eyes, and the minds of others. At this juncture, I offer two preliminary remarks that are in tension, but these will explain why I am obliged to reflect on this subject.

The first remark: I register my agreement with what is now a cliché—that all theologies are or should be[3] contextual[4] As Bevans puts it in the opening line to his revised *Models of Contextual Theology*, "There is no such thing as 'theology'; there is only *contextual* theology . . . Doing theology contextually is not an option, nor is it something that should only interest people from the Third World, missionaries who work there, or ethnic communities within dominant cultures. The contextualization of theology—the attempt to understand Christian faith in terms of a particular context—is really a theological imperative."[5]

No theology or theologian is context-less, and no theology is free from the potential to condition and affect a context and its occupants. In these regards, the struggles that I embody in this reflection with regard to contextual theologies apply to all theologies (insofar as all theologies are contextual and orientated toward particular contexts).

And the second remark: I challenge the growing claim that "the *centre of gravity* of Christianity has shifted to the South."[6]. I resist such a view because the expression *centre of gravity* has to do with energy and power. There has surely been a demographic shift, for the majority of Christians now live in South America, Asia, and Africa, but the political gravity is still located in the North. Those who have attended international and ecumenical gatherings, like the WCC Assembly, have seen that the majority of participants come from the North. We in the South have numbers but they/you in the North have power and means. I am not referring only to economic power; I am also referring to the power to be present, to have a voice, to have a face, to represent, to decide, to recognize and be recognized, and so forth.

3. See Bergman, *God in Context*.
4. See Althaus-Reid and Isherwood, "From the Goddess to Queer Theology."
5. Bevans, *Models* (2002), 3.
6. Mashau and Frederiks, "Coming of Age," 109; Haire, "The Centrality."

I recall the well-known African anecdote: The white men came to Africa and told them, "Let us pray!" All closed their eyes in order to pray and at the end of the prayer, the Africans opened their eyes to find the Bible in their hands—but their land was in the hands of the white men. Similarly, there are more Christians in the South, but the South, politically and ideologically, is in the hands of the North. This observation is not about color or race, for we have white folks in the South and black folks in the North, but about the assumption that there is a connection between numbers and power, the illusion of democracy. It does not really matter that the Bible is in the hands of Africans, and of Asians and Islanders, and so forth, if they are to interpret it according to the teachings of white men. The South has the Bible and the numbers, but the North determines how we read the Bible and how we contextualize. Our minds are still conned, and colonized. As such, the "centre of gravity" is still in the North.

My first observation—that all theologies are contextual—invalidates the reflection I want to share. If I were truly contextual, I would decide not to offer my contextually conditioned and therefore contextually limited reflection to readers from other contexts. But my second observation—that the North still controls the theological game, including what counts as contextual theology—obliges me to continue because this is a damned-if-I-do-and-damned-if-I-don't situation.[7]

RELOCATING THE HYPHEN

When people speak of contextualization, their emphasis (consciously and unconsciously) falls on "context."[8] Almost all models of contextual theology are about context, in terms of place, people, praxis, politics and philosophy plus orientation.[9] Two of the more recent arrivals on the stage of theological reflection—ecological and postcolonial theologies—hammer the attention to context on the head!

Ecological sensitivities, heightened by the troubles associated with climate change and global warming, have made awareness of and care for the environment (context) a theological obligation. How may we theologize in a world that disintegrates, unravels before our own eyes, in part

7. Smith, *Decolonizing Methodologies*.

8. Bergman, *God in Context*, 2–5.

9. Bergman, *God in Context*, 87–112.

because of our presence, our attitudes and behaviors, visions and practices, values and theologies? How may we be responsible people (of faith)
in a world whose resources are clearly limited? Ecological theologies are
of course not without biases,[10] but they remind us of our conditionings
and locatedness.

Postcolonial consciousness[11] calls attention (with voices coming
from the North!) to the causes and interests of the South, and enables
the relocation of the hyphen.[12] With this comes a double invitation: (1)
for critics to expose the cons in the theological exercise—no theology is
disinterested or apolitical—and (2) for the nurturing of *theological con
artists.* We need theological conning; the more theological conning we
do the better, for we have a lot of catching up to do with respect to the
tasks of conning the text and our contexts. If I may use a biblical image,
the field is ready but we lack workers to cut the con-harvest. I extend
this invitation both to contextual theologians and to postcolonial think-
ers who practice what Edward Said designed as contrapuntal strategies[13]
There are many contextual theologians, but not enough expose *cons* in
the theological arena or embody life-giving conning in their theologies;
there are many contrapuntal critics, but few *contras* in their works. It is in
part due to the lack of attention to *cons and contras* that the title for this
chapter arose.

Juxtaposing the drives of ecological and postcolonial theologies
makes the shift of the hyphen urgent, from *context*-uality to *con*-textuali-
ty. This chapter thus appeals to both context and con. Then, another shift
is inevitable. (There is joy with making a shift, with being shifty, because
one shift sets in motion another). It would be more appropriate for me
to use *kontextuality* instead of *contextuality.* In this way, at least in writing, I would not confuse what I am talking about with what dominant
contextual theologians address. This chapter is thus an invitation to think
of different ways of doing contextual theology. I am not herewith calling

10. See Havea, "The Politics of Climate Change."

11. See Sugirtharajah, "Introduction: Still at the Margins," 5; Abraham, "What Does
Mumbai Have to Do with Rome?" 376–78.

12. Pearson, ed., *Faith in a Hyphen.*

13 Said, *Culture and Imperialism.* See also Chowdhry, "Edward Said and Contrapuntal
Reading," 10–16, doi: 10.1177/03058298070360010701.

for a paradigm shift, as Gathogo prefers,[14] but for the problematization of the current paradigm.

Readers who are familiar with the languages of Oceania—where the letter *c* does not exist in some of the languages (e.g., Tongan) and is pronounced as *th* in others (e.g., Fijian)—might think that my having misspelled *kontextuality* reveals my Pacific Island roots. This is true, partly. Readers who are familiar with the experiences of street people might also think that I am goofing around with words, like a poor person who has nothing to play with but words. This is also true, partly. Readers who rejoice in the richness and multivalency of languages might think that I am embodying the value of language as a *living* "house of being" (á la Heidegger). This, too, is true, partly. Readers who are familiar with the works of poststructuralists (like Helene Cixous and Paul de Man) might think that I am a postmodern wannabe who embraces the playfulness of writing. This, too, is true, partly. I can go on, but these four attempts to contextualize my kontextual-reflection (*k*-reflection) suffice to show that *what is true for kontextuality will be many things, even if they are only partly* true. I am therefore making several shifts in this reflection, in this attempt to shift the hyphen in contextual thinking—this is a shifty reflection—along the line of a quote that Michael Blair, in a sermon, attributed to Paul Ricoeur: "If you want to change people's conduct, you need to change their imagination."[15] I add that to change people's imagination requires playing with and changing their language, and that they be willing to be seen as wrong in the eyes of language experts. The imagination comes alive, *if* language used is differently from the usual.

With that in mind, I will name some of the cons inherent in dominant contextual theologies, before closing with some *k*-reflections. In the next section, I briefly identify five of the cons of contextuality.

CONS OF CONTEXTUALITY, IDENTIFIED

The first con of contextuality that I want to address is the often unspoken expectation that there are essential elements, kernels, cores, or centers of

---

14. Gathgo, "Black Theology of South Africa."

15. This quotation was cited in a sermon of Michael Blair's, preached at the conference from which this book has taken shape.

the Christian faith that can travel from one context to another.[16] In this regard, theology is the wind and the vessel that transports these essential elements from country to country, from community to community.

The essential elements are expected to travel, but the excess baggage of experience, culture, and so forth, are not expected to go along. The irony here is that contextual theology highlights experience yet, at the same time, expects that all that matters are the essential elements that will travel from one context to the next, as if the experiences in previous contexts do not really matter. My suspicion toward essentialism draws from the feminist movement and from queer theory, two of the movements that deeply embrace human experience and resist essentialism.

Bevans, as he has expressed it in chapter 1, expects contextual theology to offer a new agenda for theology in the twenty-first century. I, on the other hand, call attention here to one of the *hidden agendas* of contextual theology, namely, the illusion of essentialism.[17] This illusion is characteristic of most religious movements, especially the monotheistic ones, which speak of having a core or a center. I am suspicious when I hear *essentialist people doing the contextual talk* because the context for them is just a shelter for their essences. My preference would be for taking contexts seriously, not just as points of arrival and departure, but as that which is at the center of our attention. My test question here is the simple question I learned from my feminist teachers, of which Jenny Te Paa reminded us in her chapter: Whose interests do contextual theologies serve?[18] When contextual theologies are about mission and Christology, those theologies are *not* contextual enough for me. Theologies need to be in the interests of the context before I would say they are contextual enough. This requires us to be interested, which some pious Christians pretend to transcend.

My concern here is put nicely in the French proverb "Il n'y a que les détails qui comptent."[19] I have not yet found contextual theologies that are serious enough about the details of contexts, as most of them are still essentialist in their interests.

---

16. Cook, "Unchanging 'Truth.'"

17. Althaus-Reid, "From the Goddess to Queer Theology," 266.

18. See also Gathgo, "Black Theology of South Africa," 338–43.

19. "Only the details are important." See Haire, "The Centrality," 64.

The second con has to do with language. Not many contextual theologians deal with the politics of translation and the multiple layers of language. The theologian that has been helpful to me in this area is Lamin Sanneh of Gambia.[20] The point I wish to stress here is that if we are serious about being contextual then we need to be respectful of the limits of translation. My antennas always rise when theologians talk about contextualization without pausing to consider the difficulty of translation.

My friend Howard Amery, a linguist, teacher, and translator of some of the Aboriginal languages in the north of Australia, recently told me that some of the Aboriginal languages do not have a word for "context"! This revelation forced me go back to my mother tongue, Tongan: we, too, do not have a clear word for "context." We talk about *'ā-takai, tūkunga, a'usia* and so forth, but those words are more than about context. Given the limits of translation, how can we be faithful contextual theologians? If we are serious about contextual theology, we must assist people who are conscious of the limits and politics of translation. I am not looking for people who pretend to master languages (as a translator, I know that no one can master a language), but for us to be upfront about the challenges of translation. And let us be mindful of the Italian proverb "Traduttore traditore" (The translator is a traitor).

In 2006, I challenged participants in the *Vakavuku* Conference at the University of the South Pacific (Suva, Fiji) to recognize that institutions in the Pacific need to encourage students to write in the native languages because we now have native scholars who can evaluate academic works in our native languages. Unfortunately, the gatekeepers at Pacific educational institutions still think that one is not academic enough until one writes in English or French—the languages of the empire. I made a similar plea in 2009 at United Theological College, where I currently work, and I received a similar response. As long as we fail to account for the maneuverings of language and translation, in my opinion, our contextual project is naive.

One of the related challenges that we need to face, is this: when we come to translation issues, we require people from minority communities to translate their thoughts into English *for our sake*. But why don't we learn the language of those people? Why do they have to write in English, when we should learn to read their language?

20. Sanneh, *Translating the Message*; Sanneh, *Whose Religion Is Christianity?*

The third con in my list has to do with globalization. Globalization usually refers to the way communication networks and the market link the world into a global community.[21] Globalization enables me to be in touch with friends and relatives in other parts of the world, to be mindful of the children in sweatshops in poorer parts of the world, and so forth. Globalization shows that we live in a small world. Contextual theology has the same effect, moving toward the same end: to show that our small world can, in different ways, materialize the same theological positions.

From the underside of history, globalization is another name for colonization, and both are partners in the missionary drive.[22] These three—globalization, colonization, and the Christian mission—form a trinity of power. They operate in different publics but, seen from the underside of history, they share similar drives and agenda, seeking to have dominion and to control. I anticipate challenges on this front, but I will be stubborn and say that I will not change my mind about this trinity of power as long as injustices like the following persist:

- I won't change my mind about the partnership of globalization, colonization, and the Christian mission as long as the United States retains control of the island nations of Guam, Palau, the Marshalls, Samoa, and Hawaii.

- I won't change my mind about the connection between globalization, colonization and the Christian mission as long as the United States does not account for its devastating atomic bomb testing at the Bikini Atoll.

- I won't change my mind about the relationship between globalization, colonization, and the Christian mission while France maintains control over Tahiti and New Caledonia, 'Uvea and Futuna, and refuses to be responsible for the devastation caused by its atomic testing in Mururoa.

I am not at ease when military and economic powers control the global community; similarly, I am not at ease with the invasive fingers of contextual thinking. For people at the underside of power, these moves (colonization, globalization, and Christian mission) are matters of life

21. See Althaus-Reid and Isherwood, "Thinking Theology and Queer Theory," 303; Abraham, "What Has Mumbai to Do with Rome?" 392–93.

22. Wijaya, "Economic Globalization."

and death. I am blinded and one-sided[23] in my stubborn positionality, of course. So be it. I can't help being interested, being kontextual.

The fourth con has to do with borders. I became more conscious of the restrictive sense of borders when I encountered contextual theologies. These presuppose that borders are dividing fences and lines, so that one comes to the border of one territory and needs to find ways to make sense and be relevant in another territory. If there are no restrictive borders to cross, then we don't need to bother with contextualizing. This understanding of borders reflects the immigration process, which requires that we apply for visas to enter foreign lands. To my mind, in light of the assumption that borders are rigid, theology and politics, colonization and religion feed each other.

There are borders in the societies of Oceania, but they are fluid. One of the ignored borders has to do with the spirit world, our responsibilities, relations and respect, tapu (taboos), hospitalities, and so forth. Let me put it this way: if we respect the spirit world, the values and ways of others, then contextualization is not necessary, because we will be connected through our ancestors. So what we need is to be in touch with the spirit world.[24] In this regard, the emphasis on contextualization is an indication that we are no longer in touch with our ancestors.

The last con, on this occasion, has to do with the way in which contextual theologies do not encourage us to deal with differences. When the drive is toward transporting and constructing meanings that are *relevant* in different locations, there is a tendency to omit the differentiating and excess stuff. In this regard, contextual theologies, in subtle ways, resurrect the drive to harmonize, at the expense of diversity and complexity. This should not be the case, because differences are also meaningful.

Postmodern theories of different stripes loudly call for honoring of differences, and cross-cultural theologies have joined the chorus. Let us therefore be mindful of the need to embrace differences as we relocate the hyphen from *context*-uality to *con*-textuality, and to kontextuality.

23. Wijaya, "Economic Globalization."

24. See chapter 2.

LOCATING KONTEXTUALITY

I move in this section to locate some of the characteristics of kontextuality. There are five elements here, corresponding to the five in the previous section, which I shall briefly sketch while anticipating another occasion when I would unpack these further:

Cons of contextuality ⇔ Kontextuality
Essentialism ⇔ Courage to question cultural essences
Politics of translation ⇔ Joy of translation
Globalization ⇔ Complexity of local location
Rigid borders ⇔ Enter the spirit world
Fear of differences ⇔ Rejoice in differences

First, a kontextual-thinker needs to foster the courage to question the status quo and its cultural essences, especially one's own. Since I am Tongan, I start by interrogating the text written at the bottom of Tonga's Coat of Arms, which Tongans proudly take as the motto of our island nation: *Ko e 'Otua mo Tonga ko hoku tofi'a,* popularly translated as "God and Tonga are my inheritance." What does it mean to say that God is the inheritance of a Tongan? Does it mean that I, as a Tongan Christian, possess and own God?

The Coat of Arms was designed in 1875, when Tonga's constitution was created under the influence of Christian teachers. It is under Christian guidance that Tongans grow up thinking that our inheritance is both God and Tonga. But it is ridiculous to speak of inheritance in Tonga, and in all patriarchal cultures, where women do not have the same right to inheritance as men. The motto of our nation is exclusivist, and this is the mindset that fuels our imagination when struck by the fever of nationalism. Shouldn't we change our imagination?

Before we contextualize anything into the Tongan context, we (Tongans and non-Tongans alike) should first take a critical look at some of the essential elements in Tongan cultures. If I was to do that I would end up with a long list, at the forefront of which are our patriarchal culture and warrior-traditions. To contextualize without interrogating local contexts would be like trying to fish during a storm.

The courage to question cultural essences is present in the tradition of lamentations in the Bible. The courage to complain and lament are *k*-attitudes! When one laments, one is critical of what happens around oneself. God laments when the people neglect their relationship; humans lament when God and the leaders are distant and careless. The Bible gives voice to a lot of pain (lamenting lives), but Christian circles don't give much space for lamentation. We don't even encourage lamentation against biblical traditions that are hurtful. It is precisely because of texts of terror that we need interrogating *k*-readings. This might begin with simple questions, as the one Hetty Darwin asked, which was rephrased by Marcella Althaus-Reid: Where do all the women gather if all the angels are men?[25]

Second, a kontextual-thinker enables the joys of translation. I have in mind the act of translation, which needs to be kindled so that it sparks with flares of meanings, rather than being stifled because of anxiety about presenting the right and correct contents. The joys of translation irrupt when one awakens the imagination and irritates the passions for creativity.

Try this exercise. What are different ways in which you might express the question "What's *effective* in your context?" At different times, substitute the word *effective* with other words like *cool, hot, deadly, fabulous, sexy, bad, wicked, ridiculous,* and so forth. If one was to do this exercise in English, then work across to other languages, one will enable the joys of translation to erupt. This exercise works for me in prison, when I engage the inmates to name "what's cool" in their eyes. They are always hooked because "what's cool" can be good, bad, nasty, ridiculous, and so forth. They are hooked in part, I think, because this kind of exercise enables them to think and be creative, free of the inhibition they feel with someone who might tell them they are wrong. This kind of exercise permits them to be *k*-people!

Third, a kontextual-thinker focuses on the local location rather than the global context, in the near rather than the far, and highlights the complexity of location. No local location is simple. All locations are always already multilayered.

Take the case of a Maori. When she locates herself, she names her mountain, her river, her canoe, her *iwi* (people, folk) or *ngati* (tribe), her *whakapapa* (genealogy), and so she is situated in multiple locations. Likewise, we are always located in multiple places; even the place where we currently are located is complex. In my case, for instance, I live in Darug country, but the Darug people have been pushed away by later

25. Althaus-Reid, "From Goddess to Queer Theology," 265.

migrants, and the Darug language is also a victim. The place where I now live, my context, is a storied place, but it is also a place where stories and tongues are silenced.

For a k-person, not only are borders fluid but one lives in local places in which a network of borders intersects and overruns. A k-thinker needs to highlight how location is complex, and so how the process of kontextualization weaves different strands of location.

Fourth, a kontextual-thinker moves into the spirit world. I am not referring here to the soul world, often expressed in terms of "heart languages." Rather, I am appealing to the need to connect with one's ancestors. When dominant contextual theologians speak of being connected with traditions, they are usually referring to mainstreams in the Western Christian tradition.[26] That works for people whose roots go back to the West. For me as a native of Oceania, my roots go back to my ancestors, for whom I as a k-thinker long.

I should caution that being in touch with the ancestors does not mean that we become uncritical of our traditions and cultures. This is why my first k-point above calls for courage to interrogate cultural essences.

When we theologize *in the interest of the Christian mission,* many things become secular and pagan, including the memory of the ancestors. I am denied the joy of recalling the stories of my pre-contact aunties, for I have to live as if I am a descendant of Sarai (even though I prefer Hagar). If on the other hand we theologize *in the interest of the context,* it makes no sense to speak of something that is secular or profane. Everything is tapu (sacred, prohibited), and this is one of the upshots of k-thinking. Connecting with ancestors enables the barrier between the sacred and the secular to fall.

Finally, a k-thinker rejoices in differences.[27] To bring this chapter to a close, I will briefly reflect on two Australian songs: the national anthem, "Advance Australia Fair," and Aborigine Yothu Yindi's "Gone Is the Land." I will offer a k-reading of each, concluding with the argument that Australia's national anthem is devastating while Yothu Yindi offers a healing anthem. My k-reading shifts the hyphen, exposing the cons of the national anthem and entertaining one possible way that Australians might sing if context is taken seriously. I must also add a reminder, that I offer this k-reading as a resident alien.

26. See Bergman, *God in Context,* 49–66.

27. Althaus-Reid and Isherwood, "Thinking Theology and Queer Theory," 305–6.

I recall being confronted with Australia's national anthem during the 2000 Olympic Games, shortly after I moved to Australia in August of that year, because I was forced to listen to national anthems more closely. I was struck with the first two lines: "Australians all let us rejoice, / For we are young and free." Who are the "young and free" Australians? If I were Aboriginal, I would have difficulty singing this song because Aborigines have lived in Australia for many generations, so they are "old," and their people were displaced and dispossessed of their native land, so they are *not* "free." The Aborigines of today are sons and daughters of people who are old and enslaved in Australia. If I were Australian, therefore, I would find the opening lines of the national anthem offensive.

I remember sharing my annoyance with my colleague Christine Gapes, and she told me that there is a second verse to the song, which is not sung. I went searching for that verse and became more annoyed when I read its fifth and six lines· "For those who've come across the seas / We've boundless plains to share." Who among "those who've come across the seas" have freely received a share in the "boundless plains" of Australia? This might apply to ones who came on the First Fleet, or with other European Fleets, but the Boat People, and the Asian and Pacific Island FOBs, do not experience the same generosity. Furthermore, who is the "we" of line six? On the basis of the first verse, I guess that they are the Australians who are young and free, so they are not the people of the land, the First People, the Aborigines. The "we" of verse two come from the same stock as those who taught Tongans to think of God and Tonga as our inheritance.

In the foregoing *k*-reading, I find the national anthem of Australia unfair and unjust. It does not advance the interests of Aborigines. A remedy against this is Yothu Yindi's "Gone Is the Land," the second verse of which reads,

> Gone is the land
> To the man of the mine
> Can't you see what you have done to me
> Changes coming, changes they go
> *The land is here for us*
> *To have and to hold*
> *It's not forty thousand dollars or more*
> *But forty thousand years of culture here*[28]

28. Composed and performed by Mandawuy Yunupingu and Garrumul Yunupingu

Here is a cry, a lament, an interrogation, that the land has been stolen by people who don't realize that the land is "to have and to hold" rather than to be bought and sold. The land is not "forty thousand dollars or more, but forty thousand years of culture here." If this song were to become the national anthem of Australia, it would be sung in the interest of the context.

---

on Yothu Yindi's *Garma*, Phantom 1091333, compact disc, 2007 (emphasis added).

PART 2

Theology in Particular Contexts

4

The Necessity of a Second Peoples' Theology in Australia

Chris Budden

THANK YOU FOR THE invitation to address the issue of the necessity of a Second Peoples' theology in Australia.

As I begin I need to honor two Indigenous communities: the people of this place, and the people where I grew up in Muswellbrook. Both are ancient communities who cared for the land, were loved by God, and for whom God grieves because of the last two hundred years.

All theology grows from our own lives, so let me tell you a little that is important for this presentation.

I grew up in ignorance, and so, like many others, I was forced to ask Henry Reynolds' question "Why were we not told?" I grew up ignorant of the fact that I lived on Aboriginal land and that the area was one of massacre, violence, and dispossession. School textbooks presented a very racist view of Aboriginal peoples, and there was never any mention in the church of the people or the issues they faced.

Between work and university, I went to what was then the Presbyterian Mission at Aurukun, North Queensland. This changed my life, and led to a lifelong commitment to justice for Indigenous peoples—including land rights, the Uniting Aboriginal and Islander Christian Congress, and support for the development of Indigenous theology.

My real commitment at this time is to the development of a Second Peoples' theology.

THE THEOLOGICAL QUESTION

Theology is the church's conversation about God, and how God touches and relates to the world. Theology plays a role in constructing and supporting particular worlds, and theologians do their work from within particular social locations. Theology is about power: the power to represent and construct the world.

The world in which we live—our values, beliefs, relationships, sense of meaning, etc.—is not "just there." The world is constructed and defended and explained so that we accept what we experience and understand about the world as "normal." This world defends certain interests—power, prestige, authority, etc.—through various narratives and rituals. Theology is one such narrative, and worship one such ritual.

Theologians always protect certain (often unconscious) interests—one's place in the world, who one listens to and privileges in the conversation, and what set of values and beliefs one "naturally" sits in and has made a part of one's life. Theology arises from people who have a particular social location in which power and privilege and different social networks, as well as race, gender, knowledge, class, and wealth, are important.

Recently, in Sydney, there was a report of an accident involving two small planes. All references to the male pilot omitted any reference to his gender, while references to the other pilot said "female pilot". This could be repeated in many situations, with "female" being replaced by "black," "middle-Eastern," "Muslim," or other descriptors irrelevant to the situation. The point is that "white" and "male" are considered to be normal and usual, while all else is "different." The particular starting point, the particular social location and set of interests of the church and her theologians in Australia are often hidden because of assumptions about normalcy.

The central question in Christian theology is who is God, a question that probably needs to be clarified as, who is God in relation to us (whoever *us* is)? That is, the central issue is, who is God and what difference does that make to our lives?

The answer of the church is that God is the Trinitarian One who has created the heavens and earth, who desires that people find their life in God, and who has acted in various ways in history and creation to both reveal Godself and to draw human beings towards wholeness or salvation. What makes us Christian is the insistence that this God, and this God's saving work, is revealed and achieved in Jesus Christ.

So a central contextual question is, who is Jesus Christ for us? I think that Bonhoeffer is right when he says in his Christology that the answer to the question of who is Jesus Christ is inseparable from the answer to the question of where is Jesus Christ. The issue of identity is inseparable from social location, as Jesus makes very clear in Matthew 25 when he says that we meet him among the very least and marginalized.

The issue in any contextual theology, then, becomes an issue of where Jesus is to be found and identified and related to, and where the church needs to be if it is to meet and follow this Christ. It is this issue of who and where is Christ that is the heart of the distinctiveness of a theology done by Second Peoples in Australia. I will return to that point.

The church and its theology have the task of telling a story that leads to human wholeness and flourishing. Thus an important issue about context is where wholeness is denied, and what part the church has played in that denial. Theology in Australia needs to name the particular denial of wholeness, and the way the church has helped explain and justify history and social experience in this place because of its social location and subsequent interests.

The Bible and theology are meant to be read in a way that allows people to construe the world differently. They may not necessarily tell us how to construe the world, but should provide the space so people can see differently. For example, when I used to speak to church groups about land rights I would draw on the illustration of Naboth and his vineyard in 1 Kings 21. I didn't think the passage proved that there was a biblical basis for land rights, only that there were other ways of understanding land than as real estate. There were other paradigms about land that could allow this conversation to break open in different ways.

CONTEXT AND CONTEXTUAL THEOLOGY

To describe the context is to name the relationships, beliefs, and practices that mark our life, and the narratives and rituals that construct and justify the world. It is to name who we are and from what place we tell the Christian story.

All theology is necessarily contextual. Human beings are finite creatures, not only in that they die but also in that they live within the limits of a particular tradition that is bound by time and place (and, thus, by particular language and discourse, by knowledge and specific views of the world). Hall says that this place is not simply location "but also state and condition, as in the phrase 'knowing one's place' or 'the place of something or someone.'" [1] It is both a geographic area and a shared human condition. Theology lives within, and protects, certain views of what is normal. When theology claims to be about universals, it is claiming that particular interests should be accepted by everyone. Those who claim to hold universal truths are seeking to cover sectional interests by claiming to be beyond any such interest.

Particular contextual theologies arise to challenge the way theology is controlled, and the way "normal" is determined.

Contextual theology challenges the view that theology is simply reflection on Scripture and tradition seen as two unchanging and culturally neutral resources, and insists that present human experience is a crucial part of the theological task. It wrestles with the sources of theology, and the weight given to them, and with how trustworthy the sources are when compiled by one section of society (e.g., white men). Contextual theologies are not content to simply accept the way the tradition is usually read, and to see what it means in particular contexts. It also seeks to re-read the tradition, to ask what interests are reflected in that tradition and who is excluded, and to ask questions of the tradition from within the particular context.

Contextual theology draws carefully on a number of conversation partners, and the crucial issues are who one listens to, whose voices we trust, and who we privilege in our conversations. In Australia we have to privilege the voices of Indigenous peoples.

---

1. Hall, *The Cross in Our Context*, 44.

In much of my work, including a recently published book called *Following Jesus in Invaded Space*,[2] I am concerned for what is accepted as normal in social analysis and theology in Australia, with particular reference to Indigenous peoples and the invasion of this country. I am concerned for the way we defend interests—personal, social, political, and economic—through our descriptions of the world and our theology, the way we define frontiers, and how we deal with people on those frontiers. I am concerned for what it means to be part of that people who are Second Peoples, invaders and newcomers, and how faith must be approached differently if we are conscious of our place in this land.

Let me explain the use of the term *Second Peoples*. I do not think it is my task to tell the story of Indigenous peoples, nor is it my task to do or seek to represent Indigenous theology. I must do theology as a white male whose communal history is shaped by invasion and dispossession. The issue is what one calls that theology, and for many reasons, "white" theology does not seem right in this country. Nor is this a settler theology, for this is invaded space.

There has been an increasing tendency in Uniting Church conversations to speak of Indigenous peoples as "First Peoples." This means that all those who are not Indigenous peoples are "Second Peoples." Whatever the extent of our diversity, and whatever the issues about power within this community, our common identity is that we live on Indigenous land as Second Peoples. Thus, I am encouraging us to explore the shape of a Second Peoples' theology.

THEOLOGICAL METHOD

Let me say three things quickly about my theological method.

First, Christian faith is not simply concerned for the things we believe or for a lifestyle choice in a world obsessed with choices made in the marketplace. A faithful life has to do with daily practices integrated into character, and with the way Christians enact the biblical script as an act of solidarity with Christ.

Second, the Christian life is, then, the performance of a drama or story. We are not literary critics who seek an intellectual understanding of the play, but actors who perform. I think that theology is essentially a set

2. Budden, *Following Jesus in Invaded Space*.

of margin notes—the wisdom of others who have enacted this play—that help us perform the Christian life. Central to those marginal notes is a concern for the location of God and, thus, where we are meant to be in the world.

Third, I think that the theological task involves a number of steps.

First: Clarify the issues that are being raised, and ensure that we hear the voices of those who have most at stake and who are least likely to be heard.

Second, imagine the theological tradition as a landscape. The second step is to enter and explore that landscape. One of the things that the notes in the margin seek to do is to introduce people to this landscape that is the Christian tradition. At different places on the landscape we have the wisdom of the church about issues like God, Jesus, Holy Spirit, Church, Scripture, and tradition, or the virtues of the Christian life. People approach this theological landscape from within their own context, and with their experience and issues. They need to decide where they will enter the landscape, for that will greatly influence the way they approach other parts of faith, and the weight given to them. For example, the issue of sexuality and leadership changes depending on whether our entry point is the nature of God, the meaning of salvation, the nature of humanness, the form of the church and its leadership, or the authority of the Scriptures.

Christians enter and then move through the landscape, one guide after another—one part or other of the tradition—pointing them in a different direction. The theological tradition offers companions to accompany them on their journey. They are offered directions, suggestions about major landmarks, and advice about the way different parts of the landscape are related. They hear the advice critically, asking questions and checking whether such wisdom does help their journey. Within this task will be an attempt to listen to the voices of those who raise questions about the tradition and its tendency to oppress them, who question the way that I and others have read the tradition, and who seek to bring to the surface parts of the tradition that have been suppressed. They see connections to other themes and topics, and move into different conversations. The issue is, Which part of the theological landscape does one engage as a partner in contextual theology, and how does that part of the landscape interact with other parts and shape the way into the whole? How we arrange our theological framework, the sort of doctrine or areas of theology that we use to draw our map, is crucial. For example, do you treat Scripture as a separate "doctrine," and allow things like tradition to find a bit part in that conversation, or do you locate Scripture within the topic of Revelation (part of the discussion of how one knows God)?

There are two dangers in the doing of theology. The first is that people's context and experience are not taken seriously, and that they are not allowed or able to question, challenge, and engage with the wisdom of the past in ways that bring them genuine life and wholeness (a complaint sometimes lodged by feminists and black people, for example). The sec ond danger is that people only know a narrow part of the landscape. This narrowness occurs because each tradition has its own map (and thinks that this is the only map), and each local community has its own slightly amended version of the tradition's map. This way of doing theology, of locating issues within the landscape, of finding our way across the landscape, only works if the theologian has taken the time to understand the various contours of the theological tradition, and their interconnection. There is a need for theologians to read widely so that they have as many entry points, or connections, as possible for the experiences and situations they are facing. This is the crucial task for us, and grows from an assumption which is well expressed by Hall: "We who profess the faith here and now are persons who have been brought into a long tradition, one that existed for centuries before we arrived on the scene. A conversation has been in progress and we, who have entered the room late in time, are obliged to listen carefully if our own contribution is to be pertinent."[3] Thus, an important part of theology is to be clear about the conversation into which we have stepped, and to make our contribution to the ongoing conversation in the light of the wisdom we find in that tradition, as well as our context and experience.

The third task is to suggest what this conversation between context, experience, Scripture, and tradition says about a rereading of faith, and a renaming of the practices of the Christian life. It seeks to name where it believes God in Christ is present, with whom and how, and how this new belief and these practices reflect that claim. It speaks of the place where the church is located, and how it is called to reflect on that location.

---

3. Hall, *Professing the Faith*, 33.

THE CRUCIAL, SHAPING ISSUES IN AUSTRALIA

The primary defining context for those who live in Australia is invasion. The word *invasion* is a disturbing one for most Australians. It carries the image of war and violence; it harshly contradicts the idea that this continent was peacefully settled. However, I agree with Henry Reynolds when he writes, "If you arrive without being invited in another country and you bring military force with you with the intention of using the force to impose your will, then 'it has to be interpreted by any measure as an invasion.'"[4]

Invasion is about land and country, social location, power, place in the world, and meaning. It is about the place of nations in the world. The violence that accompanies invasion is a reminder of the defeated people's place in a new world. Colonial invasion is essentially about the claims of a nation to occupy land that has been the home of Indigenous people. It removes people's rights to control of land, economy, political life, and religious story, along with language and worldview. Colonial invasion disrupts a world and the story that explains the world.

By the very nature of invasion, it is land that is the most contested point of the relationship between two people. Land holds and makes meaning. It is social location, economic base, a site for political and civil life, a place for sacred sites and their attending stories. This was as true for the people of Israel as it was for the British invaders, and as it was for Indigenous people. To be removed from land, to be deprived of access to place, is disruptive in a multitude of ways.

Invasion and colonial expansion has to do with relations at the frontier and at the center. David Chidester suggests that frontiers are not lines or boundaries or borders, but "a region of intercultural relations between intrusive and Indigenous people."[5] For example, at the frontier it is claimed that Indigenous people do not have religion for they are not civilized enough. Once the frontier is ended and people are back at the center, then it is discovered that Indigenous peoples do have religion, for such religion can be a factor in social control.

I would suggest that it is at the frontier, at the point where control is most contested, that the relationship is most abusive and yet, para-doxically, also the most "cooperative" and possible because the invaders

4. Reynolds, *Why Weren't We Told?*, 166.
5. Chidester, *Savage Systems*, 20.

need the Indigenous people. In those places where the frontier has been closed—at the point of invader hegemony and the establishment of control—the invader has no need of Indigenous people, and they are segregated and pushed to the very margins of life. Now they can be "protected" and converted and made to disappear culturally. This is the pressure of assimilation, and the normalcy of white, European, colonial society.

Invasion is about the imposition of a new order and a new sense of meaning on an invaded people and land. It is about the removal and (often) enslavement of people, and imposing a new order that will justify this removal and enslavement and convince people to accept this order. In Australia this meant locating a people considered (wrongly) to be uncivilized, primitive, pagan, and without rights to the edges of a community that saw itself as the pinnacle of civilized life—white, British, Christian, enlightened, and scientifically sophisticated.

To enforce this new set of social relationships involved denial of land and sovereignty, violence, imprisonment, slave-like labor, herding people onto missions, and continually changing social policies (assimilation, integration, self-determination) that involved stolen children and the denial of separate identity and sovereignty. It was a situation underpinned by racism and paternalism.

The European invasion of Australia was a violent clash between two complex and sophisticated cultures. The Indigenous people of Australia were a people whose culture, language, traditions, and ways of living varied between the various clans and tribal groupings. They were a people with complex social and political structures, with trade routes across the country and into parts of Asia, who had recognized ways of allowing people onto their land for specific purposes, who farmed the land and practiced aquaculture, who were nomadic in some places and quite settled in others, and who lived in simple humpies and in large dwellings made of stone, timber, and turf. They stored grains in stone silos, smoked excess eels and stored them for future needs, and tended acres of gardens. They possessed the oldest languages in the world, the first art and dance and, possibly, the first boats[6] The language that was used to describe the

6. For more detail on these claims, the reader should turn to Indigenous authors. One particularly good description of the complex culture of the peoples who lived in what is now Victoria and Tasmania is Pascoe, *Convincing Ground*. As he suggests, one of the problems with white knowledge of Indigenous culture is that in the more settled areas the settlement was destroyed and denied. By the time the anthropologists wrote,

colonial situation—e.g., "terra nullius," empty and unoccupied, primitive and uncivilized—were not factual descriptors but the narrative used to defend and explain dispossession and violence. This is the language that constructed a world of peaceful settlement, benevolence, and the conversion of "pagans."

The clash was won by a people with greater numbers and greater military strength, a people who had honed their techniques in the stealing of the lands of others in India and North America.

People explain and justify their actions by integrating them into certain worldviews, and reinforcing those worlds through stories and rituals. In Australia the act of invasion and dispossession was justified through racist narratives that denied Indigenous people their full humanity, by the legal fiction of "terra nullius" that denied sovereignty and ownership, and by an ongoing denial of history such that the dominant narrative is one of peaceful settlement and benevolent care.

MORE DETAILS AND PRESENT REALITY

This, briefly, is the context: First, invasion robbed people of their land as Mother, as economic base, as place for telling the sustaining stories, and as place that sits at the heart of relationships. Indigenous peoples were pushed to the edges of society in every sense. The land on which we sit, the land on which our churches sit, is stolen land. There are significant issues about paying rent, working out shared use of properties, and other actions that recognize this reality.

Second, invasion denied people their sovereignty. Indigenous people insist that they have never given up their sovereign claims, and the church needs to face this issue—by treaty, for example.

Third, the invasion of Australia was not peaceful. Indigenous people carry memories of wars and massacres, and Australia needs to recognize its real history. Australians have died in battle in this land. The church needs to understand that it accompanied people in a war, and occupies land won in an undeclared war.

---

they wrote only of the people of the north who lived in arid regions where large-scale agriculture was impossible—for anyone (126). We now see this more nomadic culture as the only and real Indigenous culture, and nothing could be further from the truth.

Fourth, there was considerable violence in Australia's history, against both men and women. That committed against women was very often also sexual.

Fifth, Indigenous peoples were denied their rights at law as British subjects, and have suffered very high levels of imprisonment and deaths in custody. This is still the present reality.

Sixth, people were denied proper wages and conditions, for the new colony needed cheap labor. When convicts no longer arrived this became even more an issue. In Singleton, for example, the government shut down well-run and successful Aboriginal farms because the white farmers needed cheap labor.

Seventh, this situation was underpinned by a racist ideology that denied Indigenous people their full humanity; suggested that they would die out before the superior British race (the ideology of the Great Chain of Being); and, depending on labor needs, segregated, assimilated, integrated, or made people invisible. Part of this was the decision to take the children in cases in which one parent was white.

Eighth, Indigenous people were denied the vote, and were not counted as citizens until 1967. We celebrate that event, yet forget that such a situation should not have arisen. The right to be counted and to vote is a human right, not one to be conferred or taken by the vote of other people. How could a people who had existed in this place for over fifty thousand years not be counted as people?

Ninth, at present, in areas of education, health, housing, employment, disposable income, justice, and family stress, Indigenous people are significantly worse off than the population in general. (See appendix 1 for relevant figures.)

THE CHURCH AND ITS THEOLOGY

The place of Christians and the church in this history is one of ambiguity. It is the story of people with integrity who defended Indigenous people, of missions that both protected and destroyed, and of church leaders who shared the widely held belief that Indigenous people were a primitive community that would give way before a superior civilization. It is the story of people who believed that Indigenous people were of "one blood" with Europeans and could be brought to faith in Christ, and of people who attended church on Sunday mornings and killed Indigenous people later in the day in order to claim their country.

It was an ambiguity shaped by the place of the church on the outer edges of colonial power, by its role in defending the dominant worldview (by word or silence), and by the way it cooperated with government policy in regard to stolen children and missions. It was a world that confused citizenship and discipleship and that ignored the working class that had arisen during the Industrial Revolution.

I believe that in Australia theology has largely been concerned to explain and justify, or to exclude from the conversation, issues of invasion and illegal occupation, stolen land and stolen children, dispossession and massacre, racism and marginalization.

The church in its social location in Australia was almost always on the wrong side of the frontier. We accepted as normal the priority of citizenship and support for the nation, the benevolence of the empire, the class structure of society and our place in the middle class, and the normalcy of whiteness. As a result, the church stood (almost without thought) with those who wanted to turn frontier into a conquered world, who imposed their order on life as it was, sometimes with concern for people's welfare but never with questions about the basic claims. In Australia the church and its theologians have largely been on the edge of power and influence, defenders of the major story that justifies the existence of modern Australia.

CONCLUSION

I want to insist that it is not possible to do theology in Australia without putting forgotten stories back into the theological conversation, and without acknowledging our social location and cooperation with the difficult history of this nation. We cannot speak of God if we do not deal with suffering and dispossession from land. We cannot speak of the church apart from the signs that we are a community among whom the suffering and marginalized Christ is present. We cannot speak of moral things apart from racism and invisibility, stolen children, violence and dispossession, what marginalization and abuse do to the rules of morality and struggle, the reality of a church that lives on and finds its wealth in stolen land, the way the biblical view of Jubilee challenges our life in the twenty-first century in this place.

We need to let Indigenous voices shape the questions that take us into the theological landscape, the way we read and weigh that landscape, and what interests the church still seeks to protect.

APPENDIX 1: THE PRESENT REALITY

Invasion and a history of racism and dispossession continue to contribute to the marginalization of Indigenous peoples. In the areas of education, health, housing, employment, disposable income, justice, and family stress, Indigenous people are significantly worse off than the population in general. (In the figures that follow, the figures in square brackets are those of the general population.)

Education:

- Only 32 percent of the Indigenous population has a post-school qualification [57 percent].
- The Indigenous population comprises only 1 percent of all higher education students.
- Retention ratios: Year 9—97.8 [99.8]; Year 10—86.4 [98.5]; Year 11—58.9 [88.7]; Year 12—38.0 [76.3].
- Only 3.7 percent have a bachelor's degree [16.9], and 24.1 percent a certificate or diploma [32.7].

Health:

- Indigenous Australians experience an earlier onset of most chronic diseases, and their rate of diabetes is four times greater than non-Indigenous Australians.
- Indigenous people are twelve times more likely to be hospitalized, and they have a greater need for general physician consultations.

Housing:

- Where there are Indigenous people in a household, their housing situation is: renting, 63.5 percent [26.6]; purchasing, 19.4 percent [27.0]; own, 12.6 percent [40.5]; not known, 4.5 percent [5.9].

Employment:

- Forty-six percent of all Indigenous people aged 15–64 years were not in the labor force in 2001 [27.0]. Only four percent were self-employed.

Income:

- Average income is A$226 per week [A$380 per week].

This meant that people found it very difficult to raise A$2000 in times of crisis (e.g., hospitalization, funeral, or car repairs).

Justice:

- In 1992 Indigenous people made up 14 percent of the total prison population; by 2004, this figure had increased to 21 percent.

Family:

- In 2001–2002, 20.1 per one thousand Indigenous children received out-of-home care, while for the non–Indigenous population it is 3.2 per one thousand.

Substantiated child abuse cases: NSW, 15.3 per one thousand [4.3 per 1000]; Victoria, 48.1 per one thousand [6.1]; and Northern Territory, 9.7 per one thousand [3.2].[7]

The present situation is marked by lack of a treaty, a faltering conversation about reconciliation (which many Indigenous people do not want anyway), and no formal national political voice. As the statistics show, it is a reality of appalling social conditions. It is about continuing discrimination and racism. It is also about the struggle to make helpful advances in policy and practice inside old paradigms and relationships.

---

7. These statistics are from the Human Rights and Equal Opportunities Commission (HREOC), and were provided to me by Rev. Shayne Blackman, National Administrator, Uniting Aboriginal and Islander Christian Congress. They appear in slightly more detail in *Following Jesus in Invaded Space*, 36–38.

5

Context, Controversy, and Contradiction in Contemporary Theological Education

Who Bene "Fits" and Who Just Simply Doesn't Fit?

Jenny Te Paa

I WILL ALWAYS HOLD DEAR the memory of my youngest granddaughter's first birthday party. What a stunningly happy occasion it was as those with whom Reitu has the closest familial ties and thus those who bring to bear the greatest social, spiritual, emotional, economic, and educational influence upon her life came together to celebrate her first year in God's world.

We gathered to reflect upon and to give thanks for the myriad precious blessings she has brought to each one of our lives.

Reitu has the abundance of love, shelter, and security that every child deserves but that so many children are denied. Her parents, both Maori and both with highly successful professional careers, are deeply devoted to their daughter and to each other. Family life is of utmost importance to them.

Although they live in the city, both parents consider their rural, *marae*[1]-based tribal village communities to be very important. Sadly,

---

1. A *marae* is a sacred place that serves both a religious and a social purpose in Maori (New Zealand) and other Polynesian societies.

however, both villages, where many of their relatives still live, are now in so many ways sites of serious social breakdown.

In both villages, unemployment is rampant and therefore poverty is a pervasive feature. The drug P, or methamphetamine, is ravaging the lives of too many young people. There is an appalling homelessness crisis, and the church, once one of the pivots around which community activity flowed, is now relegated to the place of spiritual and emotional irrelevance that, to some extent, it deserves. Marae, which usually also serve as the other primary pivot around which community life turns, are also experiencing uneven success in providing continuous unconditional shelter and emotional and spiritual succor for all in the tribe. Changed demographics, increased urbanization, and increasingly negative socio-economic impacts upon rural communities are all affecting marae life.

This very skimpy and unavoidably selective snapshot nevertheless provides something of the scope of the multiple *contexts* to which this precious little *mokopuna* (grandchild) of mine will be exposed, doubtless in disproportionate measure, as her parents and her wider *whanau* (family) take responsibility for nurturing her into becoming a child of the universe in and for the twenty-first century!

It is all of these things and much, much more that lies beyond any of our knowing or controlling that will impact her life. The current global recession is surely indicative, especially as its impact is felt in smaller vulnerable economies such as New Zealand's.

Political struggles over Indigenous rights will impact her life, as her parents and wider whanau are deeply immersed in these. Cultural politics as these currently play out within the Indigenous community and in wider society will form her worldview to a significant extent. She will form a view of the church as she observes her grandparents working within it and as she herself participates.

As Reitu's only grandmother, I ponder all of this complexity and pray about it each time I consider my responsibility to her.

In order to appropriately guide and protect each of my grandchildren, I know I need to deeply understand and to critically analyze (as much as I possibly can) all the circumstances, all the myriad *contexts* of their lives.

To ensure that my grandchildren are either sheltered from or able to cope with the ever-present possibility of injustice, of racism, of sexism, of violence, of deprivation or marginalization, I can ill afford to take for

granted any of their surrounding circumstances, whether geographic, sociological, cultural, spiritual, or economic, whether personal or political.

I am often overwhelmed because all of this must be continually exposed to theological critique if I am indeed to bring to bear gospel witness—the witness of the risen Christ in all I say and do as I seek to model
the faith I confidently espouse to those in my family who look to me for
example, for leadership and guidance, especially the little ones.

I share this very personal narrative by way of introducing the intellectual dilemmas that I, as an experienced theological educator, have
been most troubled by for some time. These dilemmas have to do with
what I now experience as the largely uncritical acceptance and uncritical
use and/or misuse of the word *context*.

I want especially to share with you examples of some of the specific
problems I see arising particularly for those of us who traditionally, or at
some point, or still disproportionately, inhabit the sociopolitical *contexts*
of suffering and of injustice.

I want first, therefore, to share something of the pressing issues I
experience and observe among my own Indigenous community (*with
specific reference to the interests of Indigenous women*) as the word *context*
is popularly and often so uncritically employed in respect to those narratives that pertain to contemporary identity or race politics struggles.

I do so by way of then wanting to encourage theological educators to
debate some of the ways in which, historically, the word *context* has been
either critically and/or uncritically attached to the word *theology*.

In doing so, I want particularly to focus in and around race and/or
identity politics, especially as these have been introduced into the *ecclesial*
environments within which we each operate. I want especially to debate
the ways in which various political struggles connected with race and
identity politics have been introduced/translated, in the name of contextual theology, into theological education.

Now, before going any further, lest you get the impression I am one
of those hard-core fundamentalist types who spontaneously combust at
the mere mention of political activism in the theological academy, let me
take just a moment to "put things into context."

Like many of us here, my own theological formation has been largely
prescribed by my exposure and subsequent adamant adherence to the
stunningly liberating tenets of feminist, liberation, black, buffalo, Maori,

coconut, African, queer, *minjung*, *dalit* and other such irresistible and compelling identity-based theologies!

I remain indebted to the resultant theologically nuanced discourses, which have evolved out of the deeply compassionate and understandably impassioned analysis of minority or disadvantaged groups, of Indigenous peoples, or of those who speak on their behalf.

It is in this way that contextual theologians (including the one now speaking!) have sought to articulate, legitimize, respect, and, where appropriate, transform the lives of those who have been, to the greatest and always unacceptable extent, characterized and often marred by the experience of dehumanizing oppression, suffering, injustice, helplessness, exclusion, and poverty.

We have spoken out fearlessly, sometimes very unwisely, even as concurrently we have sought to name, confront, and alleviate, eliminate and/or transform the root causes of all human suffering.

No small task, of course, but certainly it is, in some respects, far from a lonely one.

The global emergence (one might even call it a movement) of contextual theologians has achieved a certain critical mass over the past two decades or so in most established ecumenical and denominational academic networks. However, even a cursory survey of the racial and gender profile of those contained within the world's critical mass of contextual theologians will soon reveal a dearth of women and of people from third- and fourth-world societies.

Upon reflection, this dearth is not surprising, especially given the still somewhat tentative and very uneven opening up of opportunities for access to theological education for those whose life circumstances and formal educational achievements are still so far removed from those traditionally privileged.

The very sociopolitical contexts that have served and will continue to serve as the intellectual and spiritual inspiration for *doing* contextual theology are not giving of their own to theological educational institutions— or could it be that the institutions are still ill prepared, ill equipped, ill at ease to receive those with firsthand, lived experience of human suffering?

My own background is illustrative of the latter. In the mid-1980s, as a divorced, Indigenous layperson, I was one of the early *deviant* entrants into the hallowed halls of academia, in which few others of my gender, ethnicity, and social and economic class could be found!

No one inside the academy much liked or welcomed my presence, least of all those I so wanted to like me the most! Sadly, it was certain Indigenous men, who were either already ordained or were enthusiastically pursuing ordination, who openly disliked me most often! As a Maori woman and as a devout layperson, I could not understand their dislike, nor could I understand why they appeared to like me even less when I completed my PhD.

But more of the *delightful* experiences of *tribalized sexist and clerical bigotry* a little later on. For now, back to contemporary contextual theology. I want to share with you two stories, both quite different. They are, however, stories based on my own personal experiences that have caused me to seriously rethink the ways in which I now both perceive and practice contextual theology.

STORY NUMBER ONE: THE NEED TO KNOW THE TRADITION

In 2003, I was a proud and feisty founding member of the Global Anglican Contextual Theologians Network formed at the Episcopal Divinity School in Cambridge, Massachusetts, after a fabulously exciting global consultation.

We were so spirit-filled—and filled, too, with the unshakeable determination to impact global Anglican theological education such that it would never be the same! The impassioned verbal rhetoric within our new network went something like, "No longer ought theological education ever again be dominated by the 'white Western canon' or by obscure, irrelevant, abstract theological discourse developed in the ivory towers of elitist seminaries by socially inept aged white men!"

The following excerpt from the official communiqué of the meeting is further evidence of the deeply sincere, ultimately idealistic piece of what we said:

> Four key issues have been identified including: the dehumanising effects of poverty; globalisation and its marginalising effects on small nation's states; the HIV/AIDS pandemic; and war and violence. Challenges of interfaith realities were also considered.
>
> The participative and open process adopted by the consultation itself reflected an evolving theological method, resulting in a broad conversational agenda for the group. To this end the consul-

tation sought to develop a working understanding of the nature of contextual theology and its potential contribution to the life of the Anglican Communion.

The overwhelming majority of participants in the consultation agreed that contextual theology emerges out of an engagement with economic, political, and social realities that deeply inform issues of identity and culture.

Contextual theology is rooted in a critical and communal reading of the Bible that seeks to discern the presence of the life-giving God in a suffering world. It affirms and uplifts the role of women in the theological enterprise.

It is a reflection on God's transforming action in an increasingly globalised world. It is prophetic and critical, hopeful and life affirming. It participates in Jesus' solidarity with the marginalised and privileges their voices. It is a theology that fosters engagement and action.

As I reflect on these words once more, I am amazed at my naiveté! These are words that both sound so impressive and are so impressive, so sort of warm and fuzzy! Even in 2003 they were not especially startling or original, but they were certainly rejuvenating at the time. And as with my colleagues I really did leave the consultation re-energized and newly, confidently determined to ensure that all my future teaching would be even more perfectly aligned with these noblest of social justice, gospel-based sentiments and that nothing and no one could stop me!

Well, within six months of our consultation, Bishop Gene Robinson was consecrated, and the Anglican Communion is today, six years later, still reeling from the most extraordinarily violent, conservative homophobic pushback imaginable.

Doing "contextual theology," as we naïve contextual theologians had so passionately described it, was very quickly subsumed beneath the welter of prior importance claims and counterclaims that arose as the Anglican Communion was apparently polarized along liberal and conservative doctrinal, ecclesiological, and theological fault lines.

I say apparently because, as I have witnessed developments globally, I can say that initially, at least, the vast majority of ordinary faith-filled, generous-spirited, kindhearted, hardworking, humble and good-humored Anglicans simply stayed the contextual course and got on with being the people of God devoted to advancing God's mission work with deep compassion, abundant mercy, and always with kindness.

It was only with the passing of time, and the extraordinary relentlessness of those driving the conservative agenda for schism, that many of these ordinary, devoted, fabulously faithful Anglicans, began to be unduly but not entirely distracted from their prior devotion to God's mission.

It was therefore not so much that all Anglicans polarized; it was rather that those with an unabashed agenda for the acquisition of ecclesial power and authority seized the moment of controversy to achieve their own ends and in so doing effectively abandoned their prior obligation to "do always for the least among us."

It was the conservative lobby that set about causing such disruption and confusion that eventually the majority of the provincial "units" of the global church were forced to take notice, and inevitably God's mission work suffered.

It was so deeply distressing to witness at close quarters just how readily the contextual realities dealing with life-and-death issues could be so arbitrarily set aside by those with power, by bishops and archbishops, by those ordained by the church to be Christlike, to be as first teachers, those called to lives of exemplary discipleship, to lives of holiness.

One example of how readily critical mission work could be "set aside" was seen in the refusal of a diocese in Africa, under instruction from its bishop, to accept any further relief and development assistance from the Episcopal Church of the USA—the one province most able and willing to fund essential medical relief programs. "Dirty money" was the accusation, in oblique reference to the perceived "dirtiness" of Bishop Gene Robinson and therefore of all those in the Episcopal Church who sanctioned his entirely legal election and subsequent consecration.

In a similar case, river blindness, a readily curable disease, began once again to afflict the children of a certain African nation because a diocesan bishop there determined that under no circumstances would he ever allow US money to be used for the necessary medications. His objection was purely on supposedly "doctrinal" grounds, his argument being that the consecration of a gay man as bishop broke with every normative scriptural injunction outlining the moral life and that the action flew in the face of an earlier official resolution (concerning homosexual behavior) passed during the Lambeth Conference in 1998.

It is therefore as a result of the shameful and unacceptably high-handed actions of certain conservative leaders, especially those from some the poorest parts of the Anglican Communion, that some crucial mission contexts have suffered.

Sadly, since 2003, the same conservative leaders have proceeded apace to reveal and advance their real intentions.

It was the conservative leaders who consistently advocated for schism; it was the conservative leaders who approved of radical disruptions to traditionally established mission work projects, Partners in Mission, and so on. It was the relentless conservative lobby that forced Anglican theologians, especially those of us who so readily, enthusiastically, and naively subscribed to the contextual theological education model, into reactionary mode.

Those of us in leadership roles—who, while labeled "liberal," actually see ourselves in the center of the theological, doctrinal, ecclesiological trajectory of left-to-right leaning—found ourselves being forced to react to the conservatives as a matter of moral or gospel necessity (and not stay silent as our gay sisters and brothers, like the proverbial stones, cried out for justice). Simultaneously, we found ourselves being asked by ordinary Anglicans to help them respond with grace and with theological confidence to the often outrageous theological/scriptural claims being proffered as justification for the homophobic rejection of Bishop Robinson.

We were being pressed for sound and comprehensive ecclesiological answers to the difficult questions arising in the midst of the controversy. The questions themselves were still very much inherently contextual in nature but they were based of necessity in the past, not in the present, and many of us found ourselves ill equipped to address them.

For example, when, where, how, and by whom did certain moral codes become ecclesially established and accepted in our contemporary circumstances? How, when, and why did these evolve in response to changed circumstances? Why do we know so little about adiaphora? Why have hermeneutics suddenly become so potentially schismatic? Why did subsidiarity have to matter originally and now?

Many of us, especially the few lay women leaders in academic leadership roles inside denominational seminaries, and also those of us who are either Indigenous or from "minority groups," found our own theological "depth" seriously wanting, and we realized very quickly that in our own training and education we had mistakenly allowed ourselves to be diverted away from so many of the crucial elements of the faith experience of the past, those which are coded and embedded in Scripture and then kept alive, preserved, and variously defended (rightly and wrongly) in the name of ecclesiological "tradition."

In many cases, we recognized that we had allowed ourselves to be persuaded by the well-meaning, liberal-leaning white contextual theologians (to whom we had been exposed and at whose feet we gladly worshipped) that in order to succeed in the academy, all we had to do was eagerly subscribe to the view that substantial portions of so-called classical (white and Western) theology were inherently valueless and oppressive.

Secondly, our professors had insisted that what we "minorities" needed, was to focus upon the project of simultaneously valorizing the precious remnants of our Indigenous cultural worldview and associated epistemologies, even as we proceeded to bring these into dialogue with the valid and valuable but insufficient theological knowledge and experience we had thus far gained, mostly as pastoral or practical theologians!

What I think many of us now realize is that in our fervor for doing contextual theology we had inadvertently allowed ourselves to be selectively intellectually and theologically depoliticized. We allowed ourselves to be persuaded that it was not only okay but occasionally preferable to take our eyes off the essential building block of our own intellectual tradition—that of traditional ecclesiology.

As a result, when we were faced with the controversies arising from the 2003 consecration, many of us were left scrambling for the means and the material to counter the very well-mounted, often very impressive, and certainly very substantial conservative campaign.

The lesson learned I think is that the twenty-first-century contextual theology project has to be held more closely in tension with the enduring teachings of each of our ecclesial traditions. That even as we bring to bear our own earnest critique of those supposedly "classic" or "traditional" theological understandings we may find irrelevant, inconsistent, unhelpful, and/or insulting, we can ill afford to ignore the historical trajectory along which all major theological thought lines have evolved and from which all contemporary ecclesiology has flowed.

I say all of this as I reflect back over the past six years and, to my shame, observe that those whom we ultimately intended as the greatest beneficiaries of our contextual theology project have in fact not benefited at all; instead, they have been the ones most unjustly buffeted by the unimpeded waves of humanly constructed globalized injustice that cause and sustain human suffering in the first place.

Secondly, they continue to be so vulnerable as their human needs and spiritual care are relegated to a status of "lesser importance" by the purple-shirted windbags who insist on huffing and puffing their way around the globe in their ongoing and very unseemly pursuit of increased power and authority.

Those at the heart of unjust suffering and struggles—those whose victimhood and vulnerability cry out for redemptive, restorative, and reconciling action—have thus every right to wonder, to question, indeed to challenge in whose interests the contextual theology project really ultimately operates, when, as in the case I have outlined, the fervor and passion of the theologians "in charge" was so readily and unavoidably distracted and deferred. From my ecumenical experience in theological education, I do not think Anglicans are the only ones facing this dilemma.

Those few contextual theologians from third- and fourth-world contexts who have been in theological educational leadership during this very "dark period" in the life of the Anglican Communion have begun to reassess our earlier idealism in respect to contextual theology. We recognize that idealism belongs to the same word family as ideology, and we continue to puzzle very seriously about that "closeness."

We now recognize that a far more fulsome, theologically and politically savvy approach to contextual theology in respect of theological education is necessary. We recognize the need to raise traditional ecclesiological understandings among our communities of interest—women, Indigenous peoples, minorities—to the highest levels possible in order that the priority focus upon the myriad missiological tasks crying out for attention can never again be so readily distracted, disrupted, deferred—never again relegated in importance by those purple with power!

STORY NUMBER TWO: CULTURAL AMBIGUITIES

This time an insider Indigenous one! Those familiar with my work will be unsurprised by this one. The story is new; the pathology of internalized oppression and its resultant perverse/abusive behaviors is not.

The politics of theological education are, as we all know, as potent as they are in any other educational realm, and thus they are either as enslaving or as freeing as we as theological educators choose and enable them to be.

Over the past two decades or so, commensurate with the postcolonial pushback from Indigenous and other minority populations, there has been a proliferation of new models of education intended to redeem formerly monocultural, monolingual, Anglo-centric dominant models. Designed and implemented with varying degrees of state support, these new models have, at their heart, the non-negotiable principles of self-determination, cultural recovery, and restored cultural legitimacy. Secular institutions of higher learning have led the way.

Among the Indigenous peoples in Aotearoa New Zealand, Canada, the United States (including Hawaii), Australia, and parts of South America, Indigenous Maori professors of education have led the way in introducing some truly innovative and very compelling Indigenous models of education. I count my own educational mentors among some of these outstanding pioneering educators.

Indigenous and minority theologians are still rare in the South Pacific, and so the project I am especially passionate about advancing is that of increasing our numbers, particularly into positions of significant leadership in theological education. For it is only then that we, too, can truly begin to deeply and radically influence and ultimately enrich the theological academy.

Seminaries ought to be places within which *all* may participate and none would seek to dominate; where *all* are committed to gaining an understanding of God, and to speaking prophetically and doing boldly the things of God; where *all* are enabled to know intimately, to share freely and with generosity, to feel compassionately, to act fearlessly for the myriad mission facing the "beings and doings" of all the people of God.

I am unequivocal in asserting that single-identity politics of any kind will inevitably thwart this model. What is needed instead is an educational model that transcends single-identity politics, one that leads assuredly and blessedly to the highest possible levels of mutually liberative, transformative, just, and reconciling mission and ministry outcomes possible.

As an experienced Indigenous woman theological educator, I am no longer as convinced as I once was that our currently relatively uncontested models of *doing contextual theology* are any more likely, if at all, to achieve that outcome.

I say this because one of the tendencies already dangerously wide-spread in some sites of higher secular education in Aotearoa New Zealand, and rapidly becoming deeply embedded in theological education across the globe, *is the practice of valorizing intellectual mediocrity in the name of cultural sensitivity.*

This brings me to the broad and complex issue of identity politics and how I see these politics being used more often for mischief making than for peacemaking.

It is relatively undisputed that at the heart of all identity politics is the project of securing the enduring political freedom and liberation of a minority group situated within a larger context, from earlier oppression and injustice. Inherent in these politics is the unequivocal right to assert or reclaim ways of invoking those characteristics, behaviors, traditions, and customs deemed utterly unique to one's identity—in other words, claiming the right to *distinctively* self-identify and subsequently to self-determine.

Many of the claims to *cultural* distinctiveness are framed in ways that are intended to radically challenge dominant and usually negative characterizations, especially in those *contexts* where historically entrenched socioeconomic and political disadvantage has led to the internalizing of very deep-seated perceptions of inferiority.

As an example, in Aotearoa New Zealand one of the more readily identifiable culturally based claims of *distinctiveness* that is popularly portrayed as *contextually significant* is the Maori male warrior image. Evidence of this contextually significant portrayal abounds—warrior movies have been made, illustrative warrior *haka*[2] have been composed, and warrior sportsmen are its exemplars. *Staunch* is the prerequisite warrior disposition, and peculiar warrior speech patterns among young Maori males are indicative.

This very distinctive and, I believe, dangerously idealized *image* is one about which I have spoken with grave concern in the public square on a number of occasions, and for this I have been variously vilified (*I*

---

2. *Haka* was originally an aggressive form of "dance" performed primarily but not exlusively by men in order to intimidate one's actual or potential enemies. Over the centuries, it has been adapted and is performed on ceremonial, sporting and various other culturally significant occasions. There has been a discernible increase in the composition of haka in contemporary times, which gives renewed emphasis to the idealized Maori male warrior image.

stand accused of being treacherous to Maori by not being a real Maori!) or saluted *(sadly, for being perceived as putting those uppity, aggressive Maori in their place!).* Neither response is heartening!

But actually both are entirely understandable responses given that, generally speaking, New Zealanders have tended to shy away from engaging in rigorous public dialogue on matters of identity, of racial politics, and of culturally based claims, even as all of these things continuously impact our efforts at building a shared understanding of an inclusive national identity. I have experienced the exact same phenomenon of "cultural cringe" in Australia and in many other postcolonial contexts where Indigenous peoples have long been relegated to life on the margins of their own societies.

Rather than create public fora, whether in the town square or in the lecture theatre, where we as *citizens in common* can speak out boldly and respectfully of our unease at what troubles us concerning "race matters," we now prefer instead to be variously *entertained* by the antics of our most outspoken Indigenous activists or *confused* by the political machinations of those endeavoring to influence government responses. Or we are continually *rendered speechless and/or helpless* by the horrific stream of evidential data that show Indigenous women and babies to be still so disproportionately represented as victims of abuse and of violence of every imaginable kind.

Now it is within this uncertain intellectually politicized milieu that some well-meaning yet utterly misguided proponents of the contextual theology project are operating. I am speaking here of liberal white theologians, many of whom are in significant places of seniority within theological education and who, in their eagerness to act in solidarity with students from "the underside," have actually made things so much more difficult with their undue and uncritical privileging of select aspects of cultural *contexts* that they themselves neither inhabit nor necessarily have any deep or intimate acquaintance with.

It has been my experience that many of my well-intentioned, white peers—theologians, friends, and colleagues—initially endeavored to empower Indigenous and minority students by encouraging, if not mandating, curriculum engagement with *context*; indeed, social location became an almost mandatory feature of every thesis I ever marked from an Indigenous student!

The problem arising very quickly is the lack of critique attaching to this engagement. Hampered by their own cultural ignorance and inexperience, desperately afraid of being labeled racist, and suffering therefore from onset cultural cringe, my well-meaning, white liberal colleagues initially preferred not to engage (and now, for fear of the likely repercussions, readily shy away from engaging) the necessary intellectual critique of many of the culturally based claims being asserted with increasing boldness and arrogance by Indigenous and minority theological students.

By this I mean that many of my sisters and brothers in the academy find it easier to capitulate to any and all culturally based claims of distinctiveness, rather than face the inevitably stinging accusations of cultural imperialism, which are of course often readily leveled at those who would dare to interrogate received cultural narrative. It comes with the anticolonial, anti-imperialism project! Capitulation in this way, either through tacit agreement or by silent assent, nevertheless renders one complicit in what is essentially dangerous anti-intellectualism.

And so it is into this intellectual vacuum that the Indigenous cultural ideologues have swarmed with a degree of unfettered freedom. It is within this "no-go-with-critiques zone" that fabulously and often outrageously new cultural truths, even some "theological" ones, can be daily invented and eagerly distributed. It is within this intellectual vacuum that rigorous intellectual debate, self-critique, and ideological contestation are readily closed down, and instead only culturally "PC" and ideologically approved truths are able to grow narrative wings.

The arbiters, purveyors, and approvers of such truths are inevitably the newly anointed tribalized leaders, the self-appointed freedom fighters, and the courageous defenders of cultural authenticity. *Us* and *them* are thus established. Tribal rules of compliance apply. Tribal rules demand unquestioning loyalty. The gendered injustice inherent in all of this is obscene—tribal leaders, those with *real power* in any Indigenous society, are not usually the women.

The resultant *tribalism* is of course like all *isms*—a slippery, elusive and multi-layered, context-specific phenomenon. Even to begin to reach a shared understanding of what tribalism might mean to each of us is beyond the scope of this essay, but for now let me just share with you that for me, at the most fundamental local level, the tribalism I take issue with is not the life-giving, life-sustaining active celebration of shared cultural identity; rather, it is the more narrowly prescriptive forms of *androcentric* tribalism to which I object.

In Aotearoa New Zealand, this has been for me about noticing and naming what is seriously problematic about allowing, let alone tolerating, the uncritical privileging of certain Maori male voices, Maori male presence, authority, and leadership, when those voices say things and when those men do things that are ultimately at the expense of Maori women and by implication of all women.

For example (and the movie *Whale Rider* provides perhaps the most stunning portrayal in this respect), according to just one of the still very popular uncontested cultural narratives to which I have referred, only Maori men are eligible for *anointing* as spokespeople on all ceremonial occasions because it is alleged that the "traditional" rituals of public encounter potentially expose women to *evil spirits* and, further, *because as bearers of the generations to come we are, especially, to have our reproductive* taonga *(treasures) shielded from harm at all costs.*

What is so alarming about all of this is that such cultural *truths* are being embraced quite uncritically and imported into those contextual theological curricula and training programs being developed either by Indigenous people for Indigenous people or by our well-meaning white liberal friends in support of Indigenous theological educational aspiration.

The real tragedy here is that this particular culturally romanticized narrative, which embodies and reinforces the tribal warrior ideology, is *contextually selective* or even *contextually incomplete*, as it does not in any way capture or reflect the hard-edged socioeconomic reality within which disproportionate numbers of fledgling young Maori foot soldiers/warriors are actually being condemned to struggle educationally, sexually, and spiritually to find meaning, security, and coherence in their own lives. Even more tragically, neither does the narrative match the contemporary criminal statistical reality of just who it is that Maori women—indeed any women—too often need protecting from.

Ideology, of course, does not concern itself with critical details; it is more concerned with advancing and embedding its own *raison d'etat*.

It is thus the effects of these dangerously uncontested cultural narratives that I find so reprehensible, ignoring as they do at the most fundamental level the blatant theological contradiction that each one represents. It is this ideologically rooted cultural *blindness* that neatly deflects critical attention away from our prior collective gospel responsibility for acting to redress those acutely pressing, deep-seated, *contextually embedded* political injustices of poverty, poor educational standards, insecure families, low health status, and vulnerability in employment from which disproportionate numbers of Maori still suffer.

As self-respecting academic theologians, I believe we all have a professional responsibility to say, unapologetically and out loud, that uncontested populist cultural rhetoric ought have no place in the academy, unless it is to be as open to measured critique as any other set of ideas, or indeed any other body of knowledge regardless of its cultural location.

As an educator, I deem it imperative to cultivate in all of my students the habits that lead to sound reasoning and public exchange—I confess I often feel an abject failure in this respect, but I refuse to stop trying to find more creative, more compelling, and more enduring ways of celebrating the absolute fullness of the life of the mind in radically new and transformative ways. It is for this reason that I have chosen at this time to more critically interrogate my previously taken for granted assumptions about contextual theology. I still hold much respect and affection for the project, but I am unprepared to pass over the issues I have shared with you all, for reasons I know you will well understand.

One of my favorite writers in my own field of identity politics is Seyla Benhabib. Much of what she speaks of has deep resonance for me as a theological educator. Her caution to us all is, I believe, salutary to our ongoing work in theologically contextualizing our by now irreversibly globalized shared *habitus*. For even as we fuss and fret about our essentially local and national cultural identity politics, she warns that the dilemmas of coexistence faced by minority groups within the larger society actually pale in comparison with the rapid rise of fundamentalist movements, as yet (and mercifully) mostly beyond the shores of the South Pacific—even as I am so mindful of Bali, East Timor, Indonesia, Malaysia, and Afghanistan.

Benhabib reminds us that "rejectionist fundamentalism is actually a deep reaction not only against globalization but indeed against the increasing hybridization of cultures, peoples, languages and religions—all of those things which inevitably accompany globalization."[3]

And so as we bear increasing global witness, from the relative safety of our shores, to the horrific, death-dealing results of such radical rejec-

3. Benhabib, *The Claims of Culture*, 185.

tionism, and while we pray fervently for insulation and protection from merciless and mindless slaughter, I think it is true that the greatest challenge for even our globally relatively insignificant and ever-vulnerable liberal democracies is indeed for us all to work very hard to retain our precious civil liberties, our political freedoms, and our representative deliberative institutions. And let us do so with an eye always to defusing any hint of fundamentalist, conservative, or other expressions of cultural purity, of cultural fixity, no matter how apparently benign, or ridiculous, or even humorous these expressions may be.

We now live in a time and in a world where we must continue to struggle with moral ambivalence on so many fronts and with ways of effecting measured and yet dignified compromises in the cause of world peace. It is in this milieu that Indigenous peoples and minority communities have, I believe, a phenomenal contribution yet to make. For this reason, I am particularly anxious to work for the increase of numbers of *us* as leaders within the hallowed halls of theological academia.

However, all of this will require new ways of us all understanding *civility* in today's markedly pluralistic society.

Engaging with the understanding and negotiation of complex cultural dialogues in an increasingly globalized world is the challenge I believe contextual theology now has to reconcile itself to. There can no longer be any selective avoidance, any cultural cringe; none can stand aside and say, "*Not my peeps!*"

At this time, what is also urgently needed is the encouragement of informed public dialogue dealing with the virtues and responsibilities of citizenship in a modern, pluralist, multifaith democracy—not just a liberal democracy but possibly a more deliberative model for our times.

In this respect, I continue to support and welcome the struggles for recognition of difference, but only to the degree that such movements are, at the end of the day, movements for democratic inclusion, involvement, and flourishing for all; that they are thus movements for greater social and political justice for all in the society and that they are movements that allow for cultural fluidity rather than the currently fixed in time reification of so-called cultural norms such as the Maori male warrior image.

A more deliberative democratic model would encourage maximum cultural contestation through the public sphere in and through all of the institutions and associations of civil society—particularly in each and every academic institution, especially those with the peacemaking, justice making, intellectually and spiritually reconciling mandate!

It is only by engaging in such admittedly risky public dialogue, however, that we will reveal ourselves as ultimately seeking to be either peacemakers or mischief makers for our time and circumstances.

I haven't entirely lost faith in the existing contextual theology project—I think it is more a case of being profoundly more excited at the possibilities arising out of the demand for more comprehensive, mutually agreed-to critique; for greater attention to be paid to gender justice; for all to be engaged in the intellectual and spiritual work of our seminaries; and for the mediating and ultimately reconciling influence of shared truth telling. We can, we should, and we must always do a little better tomorrow than we have done today.

God willing, we shall someday soon do so together with renewed courage, with far greater imagination and integrity, with an abundance of humor—and always, without exception, we shall do so with love. Amen.

6

A Future for Latin American Liberation Theology?

Carmelo E. Álvarez

BY WAY OF INTRODUCTION

T HE TITLE OF MY presentation is an invitation to explore the contributions of liberation theology in Latin America and the Caribbean and
the challenges it poses to the twenty-first century. I come as a witness
that takes seriously the context in which this theology was developed.
As the late Taiwanese theologian Shoki Coe, Director of the Theological
Education Fund of the World Council of Churches in the 1970s, used
to stress, contextualizing theology as an ongoing process becomes a key
hermeneutical principle both in educating for the ministry and promoting a relevant theology.[1]

I came back to the United States for a sabbatical year in 1992, after
having been a missionary in Central America for seventeen years, and
was asked many times by professors, seminarians, and pastors in local
congregations about the future of liberation theology. Many times I tried
to explain that liberation theology is a multifaceted movement with different levels of commitment and development, within a common understanding on the need for a deep spirituality of liberation, from the
perspective of the poor. I heard Gustavo Gutiérrez a few years back in

---

1. Bevans, *Models of Contextual Theology* (1992), 21–22.

Lima saying that liberation theology is simply a theology that tries to convey the message of hope to the poor by saying that God loves them. For those who do not live these realities daily, liberation theology is an academic game! For liberation theologians living in the oppressive daily reality it is a matter of deep spiritual and pastoral concern.

For many church leaders, the issue was this: liberation theology is dead because real socialism has collapsed in Europe! No need for liberation anymore! With the collapse of communism in the Eastern Bloc, this kind of theology is finished. It seems to me that this kind of assertion does not take into consideration the deep root causes of oppression that gave birth to this movement: Poverty and misery as manifestations of structures of injustice.

It is of a tremendous importance to notice that by the time liberation theology was developing as an academic-theoretical movement, there were important movements within the churches in Latin America. Progressive Christian movements concerned with social justice, such as Church and Society, youth movements, university groups, Christian workers and the like, already were promoting justice and peace as key to any liberation—whether political, social, or cultural. There was a ferment among Christians, both Catholic and Protestant, coming out of the impact of the *aggiornamento* (bringing up to date) promoted by Vatican II and the World Council of Churches. These two forces were determinant in the formulation of liberation theology in Latin America.[2]

For me, the year of the discovery was 1966 when the Union of Latin American Ecumenical Youth (ULAJE), held its Assembly at the Inter-American University in San German, Puerto Rico, under the general theme of "Living between the Times." During the assembly, the impact of the life and witness of Father Camilo Torres, the Colombian priest who had decided to join the guerrilla movement and was assassinated in February 1966, was remembered. Over the next three years, we experienced in Puerto Rico and the Dominican Republic the growth of a strong ecumenical youth movement, particularly in the universities. We received the frequent visits of Julio de Santa Ana, Mauricio López (disappeared and assassinated by the militaries in Argentina in the 1970s), Hiber Conteris, Christian Lalive and others, as part of an increasing

---

2. For an interesting analysis of these issues, see the articles "Liberation," "Liberty/ Freedom," and "Struggles for Liberation" in Lossky, et al., eds., *Dictionary of the Ecumenical Movement*, 604–10.

exchange of ideas through workshops, meetings, sit-ins, and protests, particularly at the University of Puerto Rico. An eye-opener was Rubem Alves' *A Theology of Human Hope*, translated into Spanish, and Gustavo Gutiérrez' *A Theology of Liberation*, written from a Catholic perspective. [3]

In Puerto Rico two factors were very influential: The ferment at the university campuses, particularly at the University of Puerto Rico, the state university, and the presence and work of ecumenical movements like ULAJE and WSCF (World Student Christian Federation) that in Puerto Rico took the name Fraternity of Evangelical Students (FRATE). I personally participated in both groups, but it was FRATE along with *jornadas de estudio* (study groups) and *guías de estudio* (study guides) that opened the way to a dialogue with the ecumenical movement in Latin America and other parts of the world. Our primary purpose was to try to understand our political options from a Christian perspective. It was in this context that liberation theology—and originally Camilo Torres and Che Guevara—made an important impact in our theological journey.[4] For me, Camilo Torres was an inspiration because he was a bourgeois and an aristocrat who decided to be militantly involved in armed struggle. I was (and am) a pacifist and participated actively in movements of civil disobedience in Puerto Rico, but Camilo's commitment and sacrifice were admirable, and an inspiration for us![5]

Dietrich Bonhoeffer, Josef Hromádka, Jürgen Moltmann, Paul Lehmann, Richard Shaull, Martin Luther King Jr, James Cone, Simone Weil, and Roger Garaudy were among the writers whom we discussed most often. The Marxist-Christian dialogue was a favorite topic in our informal and formal conversations. Early in the 1970s, Ernst Bloch was introduced to seminarians when Luis Rivera Pagán was appointed professor of theology at the Evangelical Seminary of Puerto Rico. He did postdoctoral studies in Tübingen under the direction of Bloch and Moltmann during 1968–1970. Other contemporary Puerto Rican writers such as

---

3. To those who engage in debate over who the "father" of Latin American liberation theology is, I can say that Rubem and Gustavo are very familiar with each other's work, and neither claims to have the honor of "parenting" such a multifaceted movement alone. As a matter of fact, both agree that all the forces mentioned in this article, as well as other factors, contributed to the formation of this important theology.

4. An excellent biography, with a very useful bibliography, has been published recently: Anderson, *Che Guevara*.

5. See Álvarez, "Camilo Torres," 1019.

Juan Ángel Silén, César Andreu Iglesias, Juan Mari Bras, Rubén Berríos, Bishop Antulio Parrilla, and Georg Fromm (an American professor teaching Marxism at the University of Puerto Rico!) were very important in providing a national perspective on these issues. Living in a colonial situation, authors like Albert Memmi, Frantz Fanon, Julius Nyerere, Régis Debray, and Patrice Lumumba were familiar voices coming from Europe and the Third World.

When liberation theology was recognized as such, in 1969, it was like "good news" for many believers and non-believers participating in these progressive movements. Many of them wanted to maintain a balance between their Christian beliefs and their political involvement. The next decade was the most active, conflicting, and repressive within the Protestant churches in Puerto Rico and in some Catholic circles. Many pastors became very actively involved in these movements or were accused of subscribing to liberation theology and promoting "subversion in the churches".[6]

WHICH WAY LIBERATION THEOLOGY?

Why this long introduction in order to make a case in favor of liberation theology and try to prove that it is not finished? Is liberation theology still valid as a methodology to change and transform the existing realities of oppression? It is very important to stress that liberation theology comes out of the praxis of liberation and the commitment to justice and peace of thousands of people in universities, basic Christian communities, mainline Protestant churches, even Pentecostal churches and other movements that considered themselves secular but of "Christian inspiration." That's why we say that praxis (faith) is the "first act" and reflection (theology) is the "second act." From the very beginning, this methodological approach was useful and essential, and it is still valid!

What is clear is that liberation theology needs to respond to the challenges and issues in the new conditions that Latin America is facing

---

6. The most infamous book, written by a Disciples of Christ layperson and medical doctor, is Sáez, *Entre Cristo y el Che Guevara*. Fortunately, our friend and chaplain of the Fraternity of University Students, Samuel Silva Gotay, wrote *El pensamiento cristiano revolucionario*, a doctoral dissertation presented at the National University of Mexico (UNAM). This is an important and solid book responding to these accusations by demonstrating the importance and impact of liberation theology in the Caribbean.

today. The economic, political, cultural, and religious situations we face in 2009 are radically different from those we faced in 1969. Liberation theology will need to regain and rekindle some of the creative impetus and imagination of the 1960s in the complexities of the twenty-first century. And that's not an easy task!

Is liberation theology finished? No. But, as I will attempt to demonstrate, there is an opportunity for liberation theology to be pertinent and prophetic once more. We do not need any "apologetic," defensive spirit, which prevents the richness of conversion and transformation. As a matter of fact, it is my deepest conviction that one of the most valuable elements in liberation theology is showing the way to "multiple conversions" and new visions in the power of the Spirit.[7]

Daniel Levine, quoted by Michael Löwy, makes the following observation: "But liberation theology is anything but static: both the ideas and their expression in groups and movements have evolved substantially over the years. *In any event, it is a mistake to confuse liberation theology with liberation itself.*"[8]

Today more than ever, this point should be clarified once and for all. liberation theology is a tool—a mediating, hermeneutical device—to help us in discerning the way and providing the necessary elements to aim at that future of hope that lies ahead, the kingdom of God in all its fullness. Any historical and political project is tentative and relative to this "liberating experience." That does not mean that we just wait for the kingdom "to come." It means an active commitment in history with God, who has given us the signs of the newness of life that lies ahead.

In this same perspective, José María Vigil, from Nicaragua, insists: "What has broken down is the *model for a liberation strategy, not liberation itself.*"[9] I agree with Vigil and will add that part of what is needed is a sober attitude to analyze the mistakes and reaffirm the positive values. Jorge G. Castañeda, in his book *Utopia Unarmed: The Latin American Left after the*

---

7. Comblin, *El Espíritu Santo*; Castillo, et al., eds., *El Dios de la teología de la liberación*. This book makes an important contribution to liturgy from the perspective of liberation theology and tries to dialogue with political theology in Europe on issues of God and spirituality. It stresses the importance of an ongoing dialogue among these theologies in a changing world. Gutiérrez, *We Drink from Our Own Wells* is an excellent example of the "spirituality of pilgrimage" within liberation theology.

8. Löwy, *The War of the Gods*, 124, emphasis added.

9. Vigil, "Is There a Change," 7, emphasis added.

Cold War, accepts that liberation theology, with its impact on the basic Christian Communities, helped in promoting a "grass-roots explosion."[10] Latin America is not the same after all these socioreligious experiences that are reconfiguring the basis for new social movements in the region, in a new social fabric. I am under the impression that many people over-emphasized the "political" role of liberation theology as a movement. In the confusion, they missed the point: liberation theology is a praxis of faith that provides a methodology by which Christians committed to justice and liberation from all oppression get involved in sociopolitical and cultural movements and political parties in order to create the conditions toward a "new society," one that is more just, fraternal, and equal. Even when we examine the *Lavalas* movement led by Jean-Bertrand Aristide, we need to make the distinction between the *Lavalas* and *ti l'egliz* (the church), because the *Lavalas* was transformed into a political party aiming at the use of power and running the government. This distinction does not diminish the role of Christians in the process of liberation, as it was demonstrated in Nicaragua and El Salvador, but a new perspective is necessary. The situation in South Africa is another good example of a revolutionary process in which, once it is triumphant, the churches and the progressive forces need to evaluate their role and place in the "new reality" and maintain the necessary distance in order to be prophetic without being reactionary! The churches need to understand, as well, that there is a certain autonomy and sphere of service and competence that is unique to the life and mission of the church.[11]

João Batista Libanio traces the main developments and features of liberation theology during the last two decades in Latin America. He emphasizes that liberation theology needs a "profound revision" of this pilgrimage and search for new norms in this new context. The main option is always the "preferential option for the poor," but today this socioanalytical principle is very limited. We need to expand our categories, enrich them, so to speak, so as to make culture, race, ethnicity, gender, and sex viable new dimensions.[12] The Christological emphasis

10. Castañeda, *Utopia Unarmed*, 205–12.

11. Vigil, "Is There a Change," 12–13. Vigil raises some of the pressing issues confronting liberation theology and insists on the historical fact that liberation theology opted for the poor and for "Jesus' paradigm of the Kingdom. Within this paradigm we can find the entire minor changes and accommodations we find necessary to make."

12. Libanio, "Panorama," 57–58.

needs to take into consideration the pneumatological perspective. The lives of the martyrs of the 1970s and 1980s are always present as a reminder of the atrocities and abuses of the past. Today more than ever, when we talk about liberation, there is a need to insist on liberation in history as a struggle for life. Poverty and misery continue to be the main sources of oppression, but there are other forms of oppression that need to be acknowledged and eradicated. This includes our "silences" about racial prejudice against blacks and indigenous people and the oppression against women and children.[13] In our societies, there is a pervasive "culture of death and violence" that needs to be recognized: The drug trafficking issue and violence in the streets are part of this situation. Issues as interconnected as ecology, land and agrarian reform are still pressing problems in the twenty-first century. [14]

Liberation theology has learned to reclaim the "joy of life and its celebration." *Fiesta y sacramento* (feast and sacrament) are deep expressions of resistance and survival among our people and their "culture of life."[15]

Some of the other crucial challenges are related to the economy. It is quite clear that the so-called market economy is no long-term solution for the Third World. Some of the pressing issues and problems such as racism, violence against women and children, economic exploitation of children, unjust trade, external debt, an inhuman market economy, and the challenges of the technological revolution need concrete solutions and responses. "A Cry for Life," the introduction to the statement of Third World theologians gathered in Kenya in 1992, expresses this deep clamor:

> Cry, cry, cry for life
> For the courage, for the hope
> For the forest, for the stream
> Bodies may die, spirit never dies
> In our struggle, we burst in songs
> As a new day dawns, we will shout in joy.[16]

In an evaluation conducted for two years by the Ecumenical Association of Third World Theologians (EATWOT), it is very clear that some of these pressing issues just mentioned are common to the people

---

13. Gebara, *Teología a ritmo de mujer.*

14. Boff, *Ecologia.*

15. Tamayo, *Presente y futuro*, 75–155.

16. Abraham and Mbuy-Beya, eds., *Spirituality of the Third Word*, 188.

all over the world.[17] But the quality of life and the conditions of misery and survival have worsened in many parts of the world, particularly in Africa and parts of Asia and Latin America. Many people are excluded and marginalized completely from the system.[18]

Today the living conditions in shantytowns, *favelas,* slums, and ghettos speak of the resurgence of the Third World, even in developed countries. The poverty caused by neoliberal policies (underpaying workers, overwhelming national debt) are literally killing many people every day, due to the resurgence of tuberculosis, cholera, malaria, and other diseases that were supposedly under control for several decades. This is going on in the barrios of New York and Los Angeles! If we say that the gospel is good news to the poor, then the implications of this devastating reality are evident for humanity today, not only for the Third World countries.[19]

WHAT LIES AHEAD?

It is of a tremendous importance to reclaim some of the creative influences and "rediscoveries" in liberation theology. The preferential option for the poor was an important and transcendental rediscovery for Christianity. Today, there is a desperate need to see the implications of this option in the existing conditions of a market economy.[20]

Liberation theology was an ecumenical event in the twentieth century, of the same importance as the founding the World Council of Churches and Vatican II. As we reclaim our ecumenical commitment, let's reiterate some basic principles. Bishop Pedro Casaldáliga has enumerated five important principles for an ecumenical agenda in liberation theology perspective:

1. Maturity and freedom in the affirmation of identity from one's own gender, culture, religion, and social situation.

2. A contemplative listening to the God of Life who continues to be revealed, and a passion for God's plan of full liberation.

---

17. Report Evaluation Commission, EATWOT.

18. Sung, *La idolatría del capital.*

19. Sung, *Deus numa economía sem coraçao.*

20. Assman, *Crítica á lógica da exclusao.* Assmann combines a deep sense of "spirituality" with issues of aesthetics, solidarity, and economy.

3. A fraternal openness to all people, cultures, and religions, and honest and critical dialogues as equals.

4. A merciful sensitivity and active solidarity in the face of every situation of marginalization and death.

5. A free and hope-filled celebration of the God of Life, of the life of humanity, and of the beauty of earth and cosmos so dramatically being threatened in our day.[21]

We need to recuperate once more a "spirituality of liberation" to reaffirm the importance of the Bible in liturgy, study, and devotional life. To underline a very fundamental presupposition: liberation theology emphasizes an *intellectus amoris*—an understanding born out of love. In the words of Jon Sobrino:

> Liberation theology is one theology; it is the historical form that responsible Christian reflection has taken when confronted by a suffering world. Although this theology may take different shape in the future, its central affirmation remains permanently valid: The most truth-filled place for any Christian theology to carry out its task is always the suffering of our world, and in the crucified people of our world, theology receives a light that it can receive nowhere else. In the crucified people of the world, theology finds, as part of the Christian paradox, its own salvation, its proper direction, and the courage to carry out its task.[22]

As I come to the conclusion of this paper, let me reiterate: I find very refreshing and positive the recent articles and books written by liberation theologians in Latin America: the humbleness and sobriety is a very positive attitude. But I also find very positive the hope toward the future and the profound conviction on "the liberating capacity of Christianity."[23]

During the biennial of the Latin American Network of Commission of the Churches' Participation on Development (CCPD), in Esteio, Rio Grande Do Sul, in 1989, we were trying to design a program on theology, economy, and politics. On the second day of our meeting, a group of

21. Casaldáliga, "The Dove of Ayacucho," Open Letter sent March 6, 1997. For a more detailed treatment of these principles, see Casaldáliga and Vigil, *Political Holiness*, 165–73.

22. Sobrino, *The Principle of Mercy*, 46.

23. Boff, "Cristianismo de liberación rumbo al siglo 2." Frei Betto makes the following affirmation: Because poverty is rampant in the world today: "I still believe in liberation." See Buss, *El movimento ecuménico*, 133; Althaus-Reid, et al., eds., *Another Possible World*.

women, from a basic Christian community, came to visit and share their programs, visions, and concerns. As they conveyed a message of hope and resistance in a context of survival, and had been creative agents in a market economy of exclusion, it became very clear that liberation theology was alive and in desperate need of addressing these concerns and issues. As long as we hear the cry of the poor, marginalized, and excluded, liberation theology will be "reevangelized" again. It will have a place in the struggle for liberation in the history of our people.

These movements have been very influential in promoting a new democratic process in which people are actively participating, not only casting their votes to validate a political party to exercise power. Interestingly enough, the democratic trend, with all its diversity and complexity, is inspired by the influence of liberation theology in leaders like Luis Inacio "Lula" da Silva in Brasil, Rafael Correa in Ecuador, Evo Morales in Bolivia, Fernando Lugo in Paraguay, and Hugo Chávez in Venezuela. All of them acknowledge in public this influence.

As Jon Sobrino tells us, liberation theologians need "to realize (not just conceptualize) the realities fundamental to theology: real faith and hope, real gospel values, and something that has often required of the poor their very lives—real love. Here we have the ultimate mediation of the truth about God and the truth about humanity."[24]

A future for liberation theology? Yes! But we need to face the new challenges in new situations and keep hoping and struggling, filled with more spiritual energy than ever before.

---

24. Sobrino, *The Principle of Mercy*, 46.

PART 3

Contextual Theology and the Mission of the Church

7

A Theology of Mission for the Church of the Twenty-First Century

Mission as Prophetic Dialogue

Stephen B. Bevans

INTRODUCTION

IN MY CORRESPONDENCE WITH Katalina Tahaafe-Williams in the months before this conference, I asked for a suggestion for the topic or theme for my second talk. Of course, I presumed that the first talk would address the theme of the conference—"What Has Contextual Theology to Offer the Church of the Twenty-First Century?"—but I was not sure what would be the best follow-up to it. Katalina suggested the topic of mission, especially the understanding of it as developed by my colleague Roger Schroeder and me in our 2004 book, *Constants in Context: A Theology of Mission for Today*.[1] In this work we spoke of mission as "prophetic dialogue."

Relying on Katalina's wisdom, therefore, what I want to share with you this afternoon are some reflections under the title (to conform to the theme of our conference) "A Theology of Mission for the Church of the Twenty-First Century: Mission as Prophetic Dialogue." To do this, I'd like to proceed in three steps. First, I will speak about the importance of mission for the church of the twenty-first century. Second, I'd like to

---

1. Bevans and Schroeder, *Constants in Context*.

99

speak about mission as "prophetic dialogue." Third, I'd like to speak about how a contextual theology contributes to the prophetic dialogue by which mission must be carried out today.

MISSION IN THE TWENTY-FIRST CENTURY

In a talk given several years ago at Catholic Theological Union, Chicago (where I lecture), eminent Vietnamese-American theologian Peter C. Phan suggested that "mission" is "not an innocent word." There is no doubt that, in the name of mission, very much harm has been done to peoples and cultures throughout the world. Mission Island, as depicted in the 2008 film *Australia,* may have had some redeeming factors, but we also know that it was probably very much like the horrible school for Aboriginal children that we read of in novels like *Rabbit-Proof Fence.*[2] In his powerful doctoral dissertation on reconciliation in Australia, my friend Gerard Goldman speaks about the well-meaning but stifling structures in mission "dormitories" for Aboriginal boys and "convents" for Aboriginal girls.[3] Peter Matthiessen's *At Play in the Fields of the Lord*[4] and Barbara Kingsolver's *The Poisonwood Bible*[5] certainly strengthen the stereotype that, at least from the perspective of contextual theology, mission has *nothing* to offer the church of the twenty-first century.

But for all the truth in these portrayals, they are indeed *stereotypes* nevertheless. Mission is something that is certainly not unambiguously good, but neither have the efforts of mission been totally evil or destructive. Careful studies by Gambian historian Lamin Sanneh, Professor of History at Yale University, have concluded that missionary efforts in West Africa to translate the Bible into local languages have actually served to preserve African languages and cultures today in the face of encroaching Westernization and globalization.[6] Scots church historian Andrew Walls—of Aberdeen and Edinburgh in Scotland and Princeton in the United States—writes of the various missionary societies of the nine-

---

2. Pilkington, *Rabbit-Proof Fence.*

3. Goldman, "Remembering Ian."

4. Matthiesen, *At Play in the Fields of the Lord.*

5. Kingsolver, *The Poisonwood Bible.*

6. Sanneh, *Translating the Message.*

teenth century acting as the "fortunate subversion of the Church."[7] What missionary work accomplished—despite its ambiguity—has nevertheless resulted in the rich world Christianity that we have today, with its resulting wealth of contextual theologies to provide what I have called new agendas, new methods, new voices, and a new dialogue. Had there been no mission, there would be no contextual theologies to offer the church the new look at itself that I spoke of in my presentation yesterday. Just a week ago—on Holy Saturday—I met the leading elder of the Northern Territory town of Yuendumu. He had been taken from his land at an early age to Darwin, where he was educated by the Marist Brothers. And yet today, it is that education that enables him to be a powerful spokesperson against government efforts to take away his land for uranium mining.

However, over and above these historical considerations—and we have only indicated a few—mission's lack of innocence and its clear ambiguity should not keep us from recognizing its enduring value in Christian theology and practice. An earlier theology of mission, often based on a Western Enlightenment idea of Western superiority and a disdain for local cultures and ancient religious traditions, has been in need of radical revision, and it has found such revision in the last half century or so. Such revision has been carried out in two different directions.

The first direction of revision and renewal reaches back to the work of Karl Barth and Karl Hartenstein in the first half of the twentieth century and emphasizes mission's *trinitarian roots*. As the Willingen Conference in 1952 intimated, the church engages in mission not because it *has* a mission itself, but because *God* has a mission—or rather, because God *is* mission.[8] From this theological perspective, being a Christian means being baptized into God's very life, which is a life of radical communion, spilling forth into the world, drawing humanity and even creation itself into that communion. As many people say today, it is not so much that the *church* has a mission; rather, *the mission has a church*. The church is the particular, concrete, sacramental—and imperfect—way that God works in the world to call all people into communion with God's self. As we read in 2 Corinthians, "God was in Christ, reconciling the world to Godself . . . and entrusting to us the message of reconciliation. So we are ambassadors for Christ, God making appeal through us" (see 2 Cor

7. Walls, "Missionary Societies," 241–54.
8. The Willingen Document, 103–4.

5:19–20). Or, as Emil Brunner has written famously: "The Church exists by mission as a fire exists by burning."[9] We share in God's mission because of God's amazing grace.

The second direction of revision and renewal of mission theology also has older roots, but we might trace these back to movements within the World Council of Churches and Roman Catholicism in the 1960s and 1970s. To trace the Catholic side, which I know better, we saw the notion of mission expanded in 1971 when the bishops of the world spoke of working for justice in the world as a "constitutive element of the preaching of the gospel."[10] In 1975, Pope Paul VI, in his marvelous document on Evangelization in the Modern World (*Evangelii Nuntiandi*), emphasized that although the witness to and proclamation of the gospel and the invitation to conversion is central to evangelization, evangelization includes other elements like efforts of inculturation (contextualization) and liberation.[11] John Paul II, in his lengthy encyclical *The Mission of the Redeemer*, added the element of interreligious dialogue.[12] Mission, in other words, cannot be reduced to one element, particularly to conversion efforts. It needs to include committing oneself to issues of justice, peace, and the integrity of creation; it needs to proceed with cultural and contextual sensitivity; and it needs to proclaim Christian convictions within the context of an honest dialogue with the world's religions.

If mission *is* about a call to conversion—and it is—that conversion has to be understood not so much as a call to abandon one's culture and one's deepest values but to imagine the world differently, to begin to see its possibilities with God's eyes. Canadian novelist Rudy Wiebe says it marvelously: "You repent, not by feeling bad, but by *thinking different*."[13] Helping people "think different" is the mission of the church: to call people to work with God in creating a world of justice, peace, reconciliation, harmony among religions, ecological integrity, and cultural pride.

In the global, multicultural, minority-status, poor, vulnerable, ecologically threatened church of the twenty-first century, the church exists by mission. But it is a very different kind of mission than was conceived

---

9. Brunner, *The Word in the World*, 11.

10. 1971 Synod of Bishops, "Justice in the World," 289.

11. Paul VI, *Evangelii Nuntiandi*.

12. John Paul II, *Redemptoris Missio*, §§55–57.

13. Wiebe, *The Blue Mountains of China*, 258, italics original.

by Anglicans, Baptists, Marists, Ursulines, and Josephites a century ago. It is a mission that needs to be lived out in "prophetic dialogue." It is to this theme that we turn next.

MISSION AS PROPHETIC DIALOGUE

I mentioned earlier that my colleague Roger Schroeder and I used the term *prophetic dialogue* to describe mission in *Constants in Context*. Actually, that is not quite accurate. In fact, the term *prophetic dialogue* was how our own missionary congregation, The Society of the Divine Word, decided to describe the way we engaged in mission. The phrase was coined at our General Chapter in 2000, and I was there when the phrase was proposed. The Asians in our congregation had proposed that we speak of doing mission simply as "dialogue," but the Latin Americans strenuously objected. For them, in the context of their commitment to liberation in the midst of Latin American poverty and political and cultural oppression, doing mission was closer to engaging in *prophecy*. As we argued about this, one of our members suggested that, as a compromise, we speak of "prophetic dialogue." Everyone seemed satisfied, and so we adopted the notion.

Mission as Dialogue

Roger and I have developed the idea of prophetic dialogue in our own way, however. For us, mission is first and foremost *dialogue*. One enters into mission with a profound openness to the place and to the people in which and among whom one works. Max Warren's famous dictum "Our first task in approaching another people, another culture, another religion is to take off our shoes, for the place we are approaching is holy," [14] should function as a basic text for missionary work. In previous General Chapters, as well, we had developed a spirituality of "passing over" into other cultures and peoples. We first of all need to *leave* our homelands or our places of comfort (*leaving* is necessary; many missionaries really never *leave*), and *pass over* into people's cultures, languages, and economic standards. Another insight that needs to be emphasized is one I heard once from the great South African Catholic theologian Albert Nolan: "Listen, listen, listen. Ask questions. Listen!" My colleague Claude-Marie Barbour

14. Warren, Introduction, 10.

has coined the term *mission-in-reverse*: we need to be evangelized by the people before we can evangelize them; we need to allow the people among whom we work to be our teachers before we presume to teach them.[15]

Mission as dialogue is the ministry of presence, of respect. It is a witness, at base, to the God who moves among us in dialogue, the Word become flesh, and to the communion in Godself who calls us to communion with our universe and with one another. Some of its great exemplars are women and men like Francis of Assisi; Pandita Ramabai in India; Charles de Foucauld, a French hermit and contemplative in Algeria; a C. W. Andrews or a Bede Griffiths in India. Among several Scripture passages that I might offer as a foundation, one that strikes me as particularly apt is Paul's description of himself and his work in 1 Thessalonians: "We were gentle among you, like a nurse taking care of her children. So, being affectionately desirous of you, we were ready to share with you not only the gospel of God but also our own selves, because you had become very dear to us" (1 Thess 2:7–8).

Prophecy

But authentic mission also involves prophecy, and this in several senses. First, the basic motivation for mission must be to share the astounding, challenging, self-convicting, amazing, *good* news about the God of Jesus Christ and God's vision for the world. I love the way the term *gospel* is translated in Pilipino or Tagalog as *magandang balita*—literally, *beautiful* news. Prophecy is first of all a "telling forth," not on our own authority but on God's authority. This is why, in the powerful words of Pope Paul VI, there is no evangelization worthy of the name if "the name, the teaching, the life, the promises, the kingdom and the mystery of Jesus of Nazareth, the Son of God are not proclaimed."[16] Engaging in mission is not simply for the physical betterment of humanity, the increase of communication among Christians, or the development of one's own personal depth—even though all these things are worthwhile and equally essential to doing mission. At its deepest level, however, underlying all of these essential elements, mission is about the respectful, gentle, dialogical, and

---

15. I heard the words of Albert Nolan at the 1994 annual meeting of the United States Catholic Mission Association in Denver, Colorado. See Barbour, "Seeking Justice and Shalom," 303–9.

16. Paul VI, *Evangelii Nuntiandi*, 22.

yet faithful speaking forth—in word and deed—of God's love revealed in Jesus of Nazareth. Everything flows from this prophetic activity and commitment.

The second way that mission is prophecy is in its clear critique and exposure, in the spirit of Old Testament prophets like Amos, Hosea, and Isaiah, of any kind of injustice in the world. Dr. Carmelo Álvarez spoke of this eloquently yesterday (see chapter 5). To allude again to that 1971 synodal document, working for justice is a *constitutive part* of the prophetic preaching of the gospel. The gospel that Christians proclaim is a gospel of justice. It is the proclamation of a world of equality and participation, a world in which the greatest is the servant of all, a world of peace and opportunity. There is a long list of prophets in the history of the church's mission, among them Bartolomé de las Casas, Pedro Claver, Martin Luther King Jr., Dorothy Day, and even perhaps Sam Watson and the Dodson brothers.[17]

Third, we might speak of the witness of the church community as prophetic. Gerhard Lohfink writes powerfully of the need for the Christian community to form a "contrast community," to demonstrate to the world around it what the Reign of God might look like.[18] In Lesslie Newbigin's words, the church needs to be a "sign and foretaste" of the coming Reign of God.[19] Even if one would not fully espouse the "counter-cultural model" of contextual theology, there is indeed something in the Christian life and message that deeply challenges the status quo. The way Christians care for one another, their hospitality, their involvement in the world of politics and the arts, their moral stances—all can be gentle or not-so-gentle challenges to the world around them.

Prophecy does not have to be something serious or angry—although sometimes it may very well be. The new sense of liberation theology that Dr. Álvarez spoke about yesterday is testimony to that. Certainly, the well-known exclamation of people of the Roman Empire in the early centuries of Christianity—"See how they love one another"—was a recognition of prophecy. Today, we might want people to say, "See how they celebrate with one another!" But even when prophecy is angry—like that of the Old Testament prophets toward Israel, or like that of Jesus toward the

17. Sam Watson and the Dodson brothers are Aboriginal Australians who are political activists and highly critical of religion.

18. Lohfink, *Jesus and Community*, 168.

19. See Hunsberger, *Bearing the Witness*, 167.

Pharisees—it is an anger born out of love. It is only because the prophets and Jesus *loved* Israel that they could fulminate so strongly against it. Christians tell it like it is in the world not because the world is ultimately evil, but because of what it is and can be in God's sight.

Prophetic Dialogue

Mission needs to be done both as dialogue and as prophecy: again, in "prophetic dialogue." This idea is expressed, as well, in South African missiologist David Bosch's wonderful phrase "bold humility."[20] We need boldly to proclaim the "beautiful news" of God's story in Jesus and God's vision for our world, but we need to do it in the way *God* does it: with patience, with respect, in dialogue.

I quoted from Paul's first letter to the Thessalonians as an example of his doing mission in dialogue. In its full context, however, the text reflects much more an attitude of the bold humility or prophetic dialogue that I am advocating here.

> For you yourselves know, sisters and brothers, that our visit to you was not in vain; but though we had already suffered and been shamefully treated at Philippi, as you know, we had courage in our God to declare to you the gospel of God in the face of opposition. For our appeal does not spring from error or uncleanness, nor is it made with guile; but just as we have been approved by God to be entrusted with the gospel, so we speak, not to please people, but to please God who tests our hearts. We never used either words of flattery, as you know, or a cloak for greed, as God is witness; nor did we seek glory from people, whether from you or from others, though we might have made demands as apostles of Christ. But we were gentle among you, like a nurse taking care of her children. (1 Thess 2:1–7)

Paul certainly becomes "all things to all people," and "a slave to all," but this is because "woe to me if I do not preach the gospel" (1 Cor 9:16–23).

When one does mission in prophetic dialogue, one needs to be contextual, one needs to do theology contextually. This is what we will take up in our third and final section in this presentation.

---

20. Bosch, *Transforming Mission*, 489.

PROPHETIC DIALOGUE AND CONTEXTUAL THEOLOGY

When does one need to be prophetic in participating in God's mission? When does one need to be dialogical? It is in discerning the answers to these questions that one needs to think contextually. In our twenty-first century global, multicultural, minority, poor, and vulnerable church, the way we live our Christian lives and witness to the gospel in mission will very much depend on the situation in which we find ourselves.

I would like to take the term *contextual theology* here as broadly as I can. Contextual theology will thus include not only a dialogue with local, particular cultures and with women and men in various social locations but also a dialogue with other Christians in mission—and, indeed, with people of other religions. Taking this contextual theological approach to mission will also involve the reflection on and practice of reconciliation between various factions and enemies in the situation in which one lives. Finally, it will be in dialogical and prophetic conversation with situations of injustice and ecological danger.

As Christians engage in mission, their first attitude should be one of listening, respect, learning, and discernment. But as they listen and discern carefully, they will experience the need, even the duty, to speak out. They will find creative ways to present the Christian message and be impelled to oppose injustice or advocate reform. All of this will depend on a way of reflecting theologically that will guide and support them in their missional task.

It will be here that the various models that I have proposed—or other ones that people engaged in mission will discover—will come into play. Will the best way of presenting Christianity be a translation, a "putting the gospel into" a particular cultural value or in terms of a particular situation? Will one's prophetic dialogue lead to amazing new discoveries in one's culture, or in another religion? Will reflecting on one's practice of the gospel reveal even more effective ways of acting—more faithful to the gospel, more effective in the context? Will the experience of outsiders challenge or illumine the way one does mission in new ways? Or will an alternate way—the way of the gospel—witness to the power of the gospel in a situation of secularity, consumerism, or overreliance on individual choice?

CONCLUSION

When I first wrote *Models of Contextual Theology*, I used to stress that the book was not one about *missiology* but *systematic theology*—or theological method. This is certainly true. However, as I have developed my own thinking about contextual theology on the one hand and mission on the other, I have come to realize that my book is very much a missiological work. In the same way that Christians cannot do theology that is not contextual, so Christians cannot engage in mission that is not contextual. The way we live as Christians—which is to live in mission—is constantly to live in dialogue with and discerning our context, and correlating that context with the broader and older Christian tradition. As I concluded in my talk yesterday (see chapter 1), what contextual theology can offer to the church of the twenty-first century is a new look at itself. What the church will discover as it looks at itself in the context in which it exists is that it is a missionary church—missionary, in the words of the Second Vatican Council, by its very nature.

8

Mission as an Invitation to the Feast of Life

*Re-visioning the Ecumenical Understanding and Practice of
Mission in the Twenty-First Century*

Jooseop Keum

INTRODUCTION

THE WORLD MISSIONARY CONFERENCE held in Edinburgh, Scotland,
in 1910, has long been regarded as the historic landmark of world
mission and the modern ecumenical movement. It is important to remember that one of the outcomes of Edinburgh 1910 was a desire to
seek and attain unity in mission. Particularly, Commission VIII's report and discussion emphasizes the importance of practical measures
between mission societies of different nationalities and denominations
to find agreements in the "mission fields" in order to avoid competi-
tion, duplication, and division of missionary efforts.[1] The commission
insisted on the importance of learning to know each other, of consultation, discussion, and agreement as essential ways to avoid waste of time,
as well as human and financial resources. "The report still deplores too
much unconcerted policy, mutual ignorance, overlapping and competi-
tion among actors in mission."[2]

---

1. See *World Missionary Conference 1910*.
2. Kobia, "Cooperation and the Promotion of Unity," 237.

Two main fruits of the Conference made Edinburgh 1910 the symbolic beginning of the modern ecumenical mission movement. The first was the inception of the International Review of Mission(s)[3] in 1912 for the development of missiology as a subject of scientific research and theological study, and the second was the formation of the International Missionary Council (IMC) in 1921. Historians agree that this institutionalization of coordination and collaboration between mission actors made the difference between Edinburgh and earlier world mission conferences of the late nineteenth and early twentieth centuries.[4]

In preparing to celebrate an historic event in the modern ecumenical movement such as Edinburgh 1910, there is always a temptation to trace all the history for the last one hundred years. Of course, we have to remember and celebrate the history to learn lessons from it and to avoid the possibility of repeating mistakes made in the past. However, it is clear that we celebrate history more importantly to find a way forward. Therefore, it is the aim of this paper to seek a new vision of ecumenical understanding and practice of mission in the twenty-first century based on the achievements and lessons that have been gained during the last century. Edinburgh 1910 inspired the birth of the three main streams of the ecumenical river, namely the movements for Mission, Faith and Order, and Life and Work. In order to answer the question on the true nature and purpose of ecumenical mission,, I would like us to raise two questions. The first is, How do we understand God's life-giving mission today, and how can churches, mission agencies, and practitioners participate in it? The second is a more fundamental question: Unity for what? These questions are raised because in re-visioning the ecumenical movement in the new century, it is important for us to remember that ecu-

3. The *International Review of Mission* (IRM) is the oldest ecumenical and international missiological journal in the world, published by the Commission on World Mission and Evangelism of the World Council of Churches. While its focus is ecumenical missiology, it also gives a voice to other perspectives, such as those from Roman Catholic, Pentecostal, and Evangelical theologians. The name of the journal was altered from *Missions* in the plural to *Mission* in the singular in 1969 due to "the growing consensus that mission is one for the church wherever it may be." Crane, "Editorial: Dropping the S," 141.

4. See, for example, Clements, *Faith on the Frontiers*, 95, 101, 105. Edinburgh 1910 officially acknowledged the following previous conferences: New York (1854), London (1854), Liverpool (1860), London (1878), London (1888), and New York (1900). See *World Missionary Conference 1910: The History and Records of the Conferences*, 3–5.

menical mission is more than merely working together "to avoid waste of time, of human and financial resources."

MISSION AS INVITATION: A NEW FOUNDATION OF MISSION

I would like to start to argue the first theme with some self-critical reflections on the missionary movement of my home church, the Korean church. In August 2007, I was travelling to Seoul to speak at a consultation organized as part of the centenary celebration of the 1907 Great Revival in Pyongyang. I remember this visit as the most difficult homecoming since I had left Korea nearly ten years ago. I left Korea with much sadness after visiting the families of the Afghan hostages with the Reverend Doctor Samuel Kobia, then General Secretary of the WCC. Although the WCC utilized various channels available to help secure the release of the hostages through the organization's interfaith and international affairs desks, my beloved classmate, Rev. Bae Hyung Kyu, had already become the first victim of the Taliban. On my return flight to Geneva, I thought about the death of this innocent young Presbyterian minister who wanted to help the Afghan people. I went on to further reflect on the issue of representation and misrepresentation of the missionary movement in many places.

The Korean churches and mission agencies are sending the second largest number of missionaries, after the United States, to the four corners of the world. I would say this is a remarkable achievement. There is no other church in the Global South that has so completely transformed itself, becoming a "sending" church after having been a "receiving" church. The South Korean achievement of independence, economic development, and democracy within a half century is an outstanding case in the world, especially compared to those countries who experienced colonialism and an ensuing military dictatorship. In a similar way, the transformation of the Korean churches from a "receiving" church to a "sending" church, both in human and financial resources, is indeed a significant example for the churches in the Global South. This achievement should not be readily criticized but regarded as a model for the churches of the Global South in terms of self-reliance and becoming mission-oriented churches.

However, such an achievement does not mean that the Korean churches should continue to follow the nineteenth-century Western model of mission understanding and practice. The modern missionary movement was shaped by European cultures, social values, and world-view. One of the misrepresentations of Western missionaries was their identification with the colonial powers to "civilize" the people in "dark-ness" by sending their missionaries to the "heathen world." This paradigm of world mission has powerfully influenced and dominated the mission-ary movement over the past centuries. There was a temptation in this paradigm to calculate the success and failure of mission according to the numbers of missionaries sent "out there." Consequently, the sending church came to be regarded as the only subject of mission.

However, it is important for us to never forget that the principal sub-ject of mission is the Triune God. As the Father has sent the Son, the Son sends us (John 20:21). The risen Christ sends his followers (the church) with his Holy Spirit (Acts 2) into the world (Matt 28:16–20) as his gift. Therefore, the principal subject of mission is neither the sending church nor its missionaries. Mission is God's mission, and the church is an agent of the *missio Dei*.[5] We are the servants of God who share the good news with all of humanity, all who suffer and long for hope in their lives, and we commit ourselves to care for a creation in need of healing. There is God's "preferential option" for the receivers of the good news in this process. The receivers are the subjects who judge whether the news delivered to them is good or bad. The news that Jesus spread across Galilee was the good news of salvation for God's people, but it was utterly bad news for the people in Jerusalem because they understood the good news as a seri-ous challenge and threat to their political, economic, and religious power. They had a strong faith not in Jesus but in their money, power, and reli-gious hierarchy. Because of this, they crucified Jesus in order to continue enjoying their privileges!

When we read the "Macedonian call" in the New Testament, it is ob-vious that the subjective role and hospitality of the receivers are crucially important for God's mission (Acts 16:9–10). Therefore, it is important for us, when we participate in God's mission for the world, to discern what news will be good news in a particular context. Sending missionaries who

5. Missiologists agree that the notion of *Missio Dei* originated in Karl Barth's address at the Brandenburg Mission Conference in 1932. It was Karl Hartenstein who actually coined this term in 1934. The concept of *Missio Dei* was more substantially conceptu-alized at the Willingen Conference of the International Missionary Council in 1952. See Barth, "Die Theologie und die Mission in der Gegenwart," 100–184; Hartenstein, *Die Mission als theologisches Problem*, 31; Willingen Conference, "A Statement on the Missionary Calling of the Church," Appendix A, 53–56; "Mission and Evangelism."

have not studied the culture, history, and traditions of a given place, and who lack the proper respect for the church in that place and the people with whom they are to partner, can lead us to repeat the mistakes and misrepresentations of the nineteenth-century Western mission paradigm. One of the most remarkable missiologists in the last century, David J. Bosch, criticized the so called "great century" described by Kenneth Scott Latourette by stating, "The missionaries became pioneers of Western imperialistic expansion."[6]

While the Korean churches, then, should continue to retain their strong missionary and evangelistic zeal, it is important to seek a "discontinuity" with the nineteenth-century model of the Western missionary movement and shift to a new paradigm of mission. Toward this end, I would like to suggest the concept of "mission as invitation" as a new foundation of mission in the twenty-first century.

Mission is witnessing to the kingdom of God, not expanding one's own dominion. However, since the rise of the Constantine model of mission, the distinction between the two became vague. The result was that Christian mission came to be regarded simply as the expansion of Christendom, and the image of Christian mission became highly militant in nature, particularly through the influences of the Crusades and colonialism. This militant and triumphalistic image of mission is becoming more and more a hindrance to world mission in the postcolonial and postmodern world. Karl Barth declared in 1935 that this Christendom paradigm of mission was at an end.[7] How then can we transform our image of mission from "winners" and "conquerors" to "mission in humility"?[8]

In 1982, the WCC Central Committee approved the historic document "Mission and Evangelism: An Ecumenical Affirmation," the only official WCC position on mission and evangelism to date. Together with other important ecumenical missiological declarations, the text affirms that our ecumenical practice of mission has to be a "mission in Christ's way": "The self-emptying of the servant who lived among the people, sharing in their hopes and sufferings, giving his life on the cross for all

---

6. Bosch, *Transforming Mission*, 304.
7. Barth, *Das Evangelium in der Gegenwart*, 33.
8. Bosch, Kritzinger, and Saayman, eds., *Mission in Bold Humility*.

humanity—this was Christ's way of proclaiming the good news, and as disciples we are summoned to follow the same way."[9]

This kenotic understanding of mission is not merely talking about our mission methods. It points to the very nature and essence of our faith in Christ. Jesus became our Christ not through power or money but through his *kenosis*, his self-emptying (Phil 2:7). We believe in a God who "made himself nothing." Therefore, we, the disciples who have been sent by Christ, have to follow in his footsteps by witnessing his humility and our humbleness in doing God's mission.

Mission is not conquering or winning over non-believers in other parts of the world. Rather, mission is a humble invitation to the "feast in the kingdom of God" (Luke 14:16). Mission is preparing a banquet and going out to the streets and marketplaces of the town to extend invitations to "the poor, the crippled, the blind, and the lame." (Luke 14:21) We (the people of God) are not conquerors, but servants called to invite them (all God's people) to his banquet in the "garden of life."

MISSION AS CELEBRATION OF LIFE IN HOPE

The title of the General Secretary's report to the last WCC Assembly in 2006 was "Celebrating Life—*a festa da vida*."[10] Samuel Kobia claims that *oikoumene* is a movement for the affirmation of life—a movement to uphold the sanctity, integrity, and dignity of all God's people. When God created human beings, God's final act was to breathe into Adam's nostrils "the breath of life" so that he became a living creature (Gen 2:7). Therefore, all living creatures are alive with God's breath of life. Because of that, all lives on earth are sacred. All the efforts to save and to give life, spiritual as well as physical, are a participation in God's sacred mission. "As God does not give us partial salvation, we cannot limit our proclamation of the gospel to the spiritual realm. Rather we must acknowledge that the gospel is the good news for every part of our life, society and culture."[11] Our God is a living, life-giving God. "The realization of life, in all its fullness, including the material basis of life, is the primary mediation of the ap-

9. "Mission and Evangelism," paragraph 4.
10. Kobia, "Report of the General Secretary."
11. Keum, "Editorial: Evangelization of the Market," 184.

proach to God,"[12] who is the Creator, redeemer, and sustainer of all lives. For Jesus, God is a God of life, and his mission is one of giving life (John 10:10; 14:6). According to K. C. Abraham, his messianic signs are signs of life in its fullness. "To believe in God is to affirm the supremacy of life over death."[13] "This also means any assault of life—hunger, destitution, squalor, oppression, and injustice—is an attack on God, on God's will for the life of humankind. A denial of life, therefore, is a rejection of the God of life."[14] Jürgen Moltmann writes, "Where Jesus is, there is life. There is abundant life, vigorous life, loved life and eternal life."[15] Indeed, our mission is to follow this life-saving and life-giving mission of Christ and to witness to the abundant life in word and deed.

We live in a world where this sacred God-given life is at stake. For instance, the current global economic crisis is a man-made disaster detrimental to both humanity and creation. As early as the Harare Assembly in 1998, the WCC had warned the global financial institutions, such as the IMF, World Bank, and WTO, and the OECD countries, through the AGAPE Process,[16] that neoliberal economic globalization is not sustainable and is one of the most serious life-threatening forces today. However, people did not listen carefully to the prophetic voices, possibly because they were enjoying the benefits of the crises in the Asian markets at that time. Within a decade, we are listening again to the cries of the people who have lost their jobs, houses, and pensions because of the greedy hands of "casino capitalism." This time, however, the cries come from the United States and countries in the EU that were the beneficiaries of the Asian crisis ten years ago. Everything is connected, as we know.

However, we should not forget that the impact of the current economic crisis is becoming a life-and-death matter for the people of the Global South, where there is a lack of social security. The global scale of economic dictatorship by the neoliberal market is causing the "genocide" of creation and the environment, as well. Neoliberal economic globalization comes with a strong ideological dimension, or a quasi-religious mes-

---

12. Sobrino, "The Epiphany," 73.

13. Abraham, "Mission as Celebration of Life," 31.

14. Gustavo Gutiérrez, as quoted in Araya, *God of the Poor*, 73.

15. Moltmann, *The Passion for Life*, 22.

16. Concerning the AGAPE Process, see Mshana, ed., *Alternative Globalization*.

sage along the lines of, "The global market system will save the world."[17] It is not only a threat to economic life but also to the spiritual life of people.[18]

This is why the WCC and WARC[19] (World Alliance of Reformed Churches) have taken a faith stance in economic issues of globalization. Indeed, "Christian contributions to public debate are, or ought to be, a way of confessing the faith, a part of the mission of the church, a form of evangelism."[20] Throughout the world, we Christians should be able to confess our faith with regards to economic issues, and we believe that this should be done through the mission and spiritual life of the church.[21] This is especially true when life is the issue in question. The church has to take a firm stance on life issues because we believe it is the most powerful action the faith community can take.[22]

How then can we reclaim mission to be life affirming in the context of global economic crisis? How can we celebrate life in the midst of news of wars, disasters, and crises? Celebrating life in this situation means bringing an eschatological hope to the horizon of history. Duncan B. Forrester states, "Hope is resistance to a hopeless situation. Hope keeps open the horizon of the future and motivates action . . . Our faith in a New Heaven and a New Earth gives substance to hope, shapes and sustains hope. This hope is at its heart and throughout social. The hope is good news to the poor and all who suffer."[23]

This hope challenges the existing order of injustice and structural evil. The bankruptcy of hope never existed in Jesus and his mission. Hope is an inescapable way of envisioning the future. "Where there is no vision the people perish"(Prov 29:18). Therefore, our mission is celebrating life with the hope that another world is possible. Our mission is to prepare the feast of life and to invite all God's peoples to this fiesta. In the midst of agonies, despair, and cries of the pain of life, it is our mission to seek alternative values, ways of life and communities to actualize the kingdom of God on earth.

---

17. See Hayek, *Law, Legislation and Liberty*, 63–70.

18. Keum, "Editorial: Evangelization of the Market," 183–84.

19. Concerning WARC's work on the issue, see Park, ed., *Reformed World*.

20. Forrester, "Mission in the Public Square," 1.

21. Biéler, *Calvin's Economic and Social Thought*, 304–9.

22. Keum, "Take Home the Good News," 28.

23. Forrester, *Christian Justice*, 246–47.

TRANSFORMATIVE SPIRITUALITY IN MISSION

What is our basis in our participation in God's life-giving mission? Kobia answers, "As a Christian, I discern the gift of God's grace when life is transformed and hope becomes reality. It is against such a backdrop that I dream of an ecumenical movement of people who are messengers of God's grace, a people open to each other and discovering the presence of Christ and of God's grace in the other. To see Christ in the other is so much stronger than all that separates us."[24]

The theme of the last WCC Assembly was "God in your grace, transform the world."[25] We have learned through the Assembly that while the global ecumenical movement is struggling to find a new source of energy, the people and faith communities in grassroots communities have firmly rooted their feet in God's transformative grace as a source of life. During the last century, the modern ecumenical movement has developed within the philosophical framework of Western modernism and rationalism. Therefore, ecumenism has been forced to work on a "logical" basis. In other words, we have sought the foundation of the ecumenical movement in *ideo*-logical or *theo*-logical bases. However, it is time to shift the foundation of the ecumenical movement from such a rational basis to a spiritual one. I suggest an ecumenical movement that is firmly grounded in "spirituality" as the feast of life.[26] If the *logos* was the basis of ecumenism in the twentieth century, *pneuma* will be its basis in the twenty-first century.

I have reached this conclusion through the reading of two distinctive signs of the times in today's world, one secular and the other ecclesiastical. The first sign is the rise of a global civil movement and the second is the shift in the center of world Christianity. Firstly, I would like to draw your attention to the methodology employed in organizing the World Social Forum (WSF) by the global civil movement. It is not a movement with a strongly institutionalized center, but a "movement of movements."[27] While the social movements were based on strong sociopolitical and socioeconomic ideologies during the last century, it is spirituality that binds the different movements together at a global level

---

24. Kobia, *Called to One Hope*, 1–2.

25. Rivera-Pagán, ed., *God in Your Grace*.

26. Kobia, "Report of the General Secretary," 2.

27. Leite, *The World Social Forum*.

in the space of the WSF. Even the slogan "Another world is possible!" sounds like a strong spiritual and prophetic message and seems to be grounded on faith values. It was a surprising experience when the WCC team on Economic Justice organized the workshop titled "Spiritual Basis of Christian Participation in Social Issues" during the Nairobi WSF in 2007. Indeed, it was one of the most popular workshops among all the seminar programs during the forum. Certainly, there is a yearning for spirituality in the global civil society. Spirituality can facilitate a dialogue between the mission of the church and the most prophetic voices in the world today. While we share our spiritual resources with the civil movements we could also learn from them what the most urgent mission priorities are in the contemporary world.

To mobilize and build the global alternative movement, it is necessary that resources for spiritual renewal be developed as an essential basis of the movement. Spirituality is the core of why we do what we do and how we live, that which gives our lives deepest meaning and stimulates, motivates, and gives dynamism to life's journey. "It is energy for life in all its fullness and calls for a commitment to resist all forces, powers and systems which reduce, deny or destroy life. It reveals to us a deepening sense of the God who cares for all living things. It is the praxis of affirming and caring for life as a sacred gift from the Creator which is being sustained in as much as it is being shared in community."[28]

On the other hand, we can read a clear ecclesiastical sign that the center of world Christianity has moved to the churches of the Global South. More than 65 percent of the world's Christian populations live in Asia, Africa, and Latin America today.[29] This change of global Christian demography will bring a new ecumenical landscape sooner rather than later. The twentieth century's modernistic paradigm of ecumenism has been challenged to reformulate its ecumenical agenda and reshape its leadership.

Among the several impacts of this paradigm shift, I would like again to point out the importance of the spiritual basis of the ecumenical and missional movement. The manner in which the ecumenical movements in the Christian South address ecumenical and mission agendas is not always done according to rational logic, nor is it simply based on scientific analysis. Rather, their methodology seeks to address the issue of

---

28. WCC, WARC, and CWM, "Report of the *Oikotree* Consultation," 1. See also Groody, *Globalization*.

29. See Walls, *The Missionary Movement*; Jenkins, *The Next Christendom*.

life directly from its daily context, finds divine insights through spiritual discernment, and acts on that insight through the power of the Holy Spirit. Jung Woon Suh clarified the co-relationship between the growth of Christianity in the non-Western world and spirituality with a case study of the Korean church. As he put it, the "Korean church, from its beginning, experienced poverty, oppression, pain and suffering and its spirituality has been formed through such life experiences. Sorrow and pain are woven into the spirituality of the Korean church.[30]

We must seriously consider and work out ways in which we can re-formulate our ecumenical and missional agenda, structure, and working style in order to bring the concerns of the majority of world Christianity to the heart of the ecumenical movement. In the search for a new ecu-menism, the dialogue with the mission issues of the Global South has to be one of most important parts of the church's work. At the center of this process is an emphasis on spirituality.

In Edinburgh 1910, my first predecessor, Joseph H. Oldham, recog-nized that it was essential to develop institutions to secure the ecumeni-cal movement. Therefore, the Edinburgh Continuation Committee was formed and became the womb for the birth of the IMC and WCC. After a century of the institutionalization of the ecumenical missionary move-ment, I find that the temptation always exists for institutions to serve only their self-interests. "The ecumenical movement must remain a ferment of change, recovering the spirit that led it to take risks."[31] Indeed, mission is the taking of risks to give life to suffering people,[32] and eventually to transform the world to the kingdom of God. Therefore, it is important to articulate a transforming ecumenism through a mission-centered ap-proach that will inspire institutionalized ecumenism at this particular juncture of history in the ecumenical movement.

The former WCC General Secretary, the Reverend Doctor Konrad Raiser, suggested the notion of a "spirituality of resistance" as a basis for the church's participation in prophetic witness.[33] In line with his contribu-tion, I would like to suggest a "spirituality of transformation" as a founda-tion for ecumenical mission in the twenty-first century. "Resistance" is

30. Suh, *Spirituality and Theology in Mission*, 4–6.
31. Kobia, "Listening to the Voice of God," 9.
32. Suh, *Spirituality and Theology in Mission*, 6–8.
33. Raiser, "Spirituality of Resistance."

the first step in speaking out about the sufferings of people and in de-
molishing the structures of evil. However, there is still the crucial task
of transforming the structure by presenting alternatives to the existing
world mechanism. Transformation compels us, as churches, to move
beyond the difficult but conceivable to imagine, discover, embrace, and
embody the truly liberating, and then to make that liberation possible.[34]
Transformative spirituality is a spirituality that provides inspiration and
creativity to imagine another possible world, and energizes humanity to
live out our new vision of the earth community. Indeed, the ecumenical
movement must remain a radical change to recover the spirit that led our
forbears to dare to take risks.

FROM MOUNTAIN TO VALLEY

Talking about the interfaith issue is tricky and even demands courage
in some contexts. Before articulating my thesis on interfaith dialogue,
I would like to remind you that the only official mission statement approved by the WCC Central Committee in 1982 affirmed the uniqueness
of Jesus Christ.[35] There are some misunderstandings of WCC's position
with regard to interfaith issues, mainly because of the failure to distinguish between personal positions taken by individuals who were invited
as speakers and the official position of the WCC.[36] I would like to boldly
speak on the issue of interfaith dialogue today because it is a highly important mission agenda in the twenty-first century.

A decade ago, the whole world was celebrating the new millennium
with a rosy dream of a new chapter of human history. There were many
who were full of optimism for human history and expectations that the
new millennium would be different from the previous two. It seemed that
we created beings could finally overcome our limitations and become
"creators" through unveiling the mysteries of life. However, even before

34. Mshana, *Alternative Globalization*, 37.

35. "Mission and Evangelism," paragraph 41.

36. Recently, there has been a discussion in the Holiness Church in Korea about re-
newing its membership with the National Council of Churches in Korea and the World
Council of Churches. Those people who oppose this development justify keeping the
status quo because the WCC accepts religious pluralism. See *The Kookmin Daily*. Such a
charge, however, is totally untrue. The WCC has never acknowledged a pluralist understanding of religions in its official understanding of mission.

the Millennium Tower started to function, the news of terrorism, crises, wars, and disasters were endlessly reported by the media. It was inevitable that a fundamental doubt regarding the moral capacity of human beings arose as a consequence. It did not take a decade to reaffirm the sinful nature of human beings who have the capacity to destroy the God-created world. How far away we have moved from the vision that our Creator originally intended for the *oikoumene*. The world seems to have sunk deeper into the spiral of violence in recent years. There are women, children, and men all over the world suffering from many forms of violence—terror, abuse, torture, and extreme poverty. Peace today seems very far away.

In the face of this extreme violence in the world, religions have taken the old "emperor's new clothes" approach, in some cases. Moreover, numerous acts of violence, terrorism, and even genocide have been fueled by religionists. Some could argue that it was politicians who actually caused the conflicts and justified them in the name of religion. Even so, there remains the question, Can we refuse to admire the emperor's clothes and instead cry out, like the little boy in the tale, "But the emperor has no clothes on!"?[37] During his visit to the WCC on 3 March 2008, UN Secretary-General Ban Ki-moon suggested that the two international organizations work more closely on global issues, particularly on peace and climate change. He asked the WCC to bring together the world's religious leaders and facilitate dialogue on those issues. Missiologists are being called to respond to these global demands of interfaith encounter in the new century.

Many of us are familiar with the analogy that God is the top of a mountain and there are many pathways that lead to the truth. However, are we really climbing the same mountain? The concept of and belief in salvation is unique and exists only within Christianity. The Buddhist understanding of nirvana is totally different from Christian salvation. According to Mark Heim, in fact, we are climbing different mountains, and the truths that could be found at the top are not all the same.[38] Those who believe that we can reach the top in only one way we label exclusivists; those who believe in many ways, universalists; and those who believe in many mountains, pluralists. Furthermore, the theological ar-

---

37. Forrester, "Mission in the Public Square," 17.
38. Heim, *Salvations*. See also his *The Depth of the Riches*.

gument on this issue became a discipline, namely theology of religion, whether in conservative or progressive schools with different purposes and methodologies.

Here, I would like to suggest a pilgrimage of climbing down from the mountain to the valley, from interfaith dialogue to interfaith cooperation. As long as we stay at the top of the mountain, we cannot meet, listen, dialogue, and work together for and with the people who struggle daily to survive, including people of other faiths, because the top is too high for ordinary people to climb and the path too narrow for them to stay on. If we are climbing different mountains, as Heim claims, how can we listen to each other, meet face-to-face, and talk together at the top of different mountains? We are too far away from each other to listen, meet, and talk. It is an impossible task to work together while we are sitting on different and remote mountaintops. In fact, it is in the valley, not at the mountaintop, where we can meet people of other faiths. It is in the valley where we can live in a community and where we can live out the truth. Indeed, when Peter insisted that he and Jesus, along with James and John, live forever on the top of the Mountain of Transfiguration because "it was so good that they were there," Jesus taught Peter to go down to the valley where the villages were located (Luke 9:33). In many religious traditions in both the East and the West, the mountain represents sacred religious space for spiritual discipline. But, no matter how "good" it was to receive the truth from heaven at Mount Sinai, or to listen to the heavenly voice at the Mount of Transfiguration, Jesus never allowed his disciples to stay there forever. Jesus said, "Stand up, do not be afraid" (Matt 17:7) to go down to the valley where people were inheriting households and waiting for some good news. As soon as they came back to the community, the disciples were met by the father whose son was an epileptic, and their mission began (Matt 17:15).

The direction of missionary movement is not climbing up to the mountain but rather going down to the valley. We believe in an incarnated God, the Son of Man, who voluntarily gave up his heavenly position and became a missionary servant to wash our feet. It is this God whom we believe in as our Christian God. An authentic missionary journey in interfaith dialogue can be achieved when we follow the direction of God's missionary journey from heaven to earth, of Jesus' journey from mountain to valley. Having served in different mission organizations, I have faced a similar situation during my mission travels to that faced by Peter after his journey to the Mountain of Transfiguration. In North Korea, I saw a baby dying of hunger. In such a situation, I would never ask the religious background of the person beside me to discern whether we are allowed to work together to save the baby or not! It is time for mission to climb down from the Ivory Tower of interfaith mountains and to seek to cooperate in bringing peace and life into the world.

PEACE AND RECONCILIATION

The theme of the thirteenth WCC Conference on World Mission and Evangelism, held in Athens in 2005, was "Come Holy Spirit, Heal and Reconcile."[39] The message sent out from Athens to the churches and mission organizations emphasizes the importance of the ministry of healing and reconciliation:

> We stand now at a particular moment in the history of mission. While the centers of power are still predominantly in the global North, it is in the South and East that the churches are growing most rapidly, as a result of faithful Christian mission and witness. The missional character of the Church is experienced in greater diversity than ever, as the Christian communities continue the search for distinctive response to the Gospel. The diversity is challenging, and it should sometimes make us uneasy. Nevertheless, within it we have discovered opportunities for deepening understanding of the Holy Spirit's creative, life-sustaining, healing and reconciling work . . . But there are evil spirits too, active in the world and sadly even in many of our histories and communities. These are spirits of violence, oppression, exclusion, division, corruption, self-seeking, ignorance, failure to live up to our beliefs and of fearful silence in the face of injustice . . . In Athens we were aware of the new challenges that come from the need for reconciliation between East and West, North and South, and between Christians and people of other faiths.[40]

The letter quotes the missionary message of Paul, "God was reconciling the world to himself, not counting their trespasses against them, and entrusting the message of reconciliation to us. So we are ambassadors for Christ, since God is making his appeal through us; we entrust you on

39. See Matthey, ed., *Come Holy Spirit*.
40. "A Letter," in Matthey, ed., *Come Holy Spirit*, 324.

behalf of Christ, be reconciled to God." (2 Cor 5:19–20) It is this "new creation" that we hold to be the goal of our missionary endeavor. "We believe that reconciliation and healing are pivotal to the progress by which that goal is to be reached. Reconciliation, as the restoration of right relations with God, is the source of reconciliation with oneself, with other people and with the whole creation."[41]

As people of faith, we cannot close our eyes to reality. Nor should we despair—we can still believe in the power and the promise of reconciliation as an alternative to violence and divisions. Kosuke Koyama writes, "The unique and awesome truth about human history is that it can become creative or destructive, healing or damaging because at its basis there is a mysterious freedom of human confidence and faith of the heart which can make both God and idol. This is the risk that the creator God took."[42]

Jesus attempted to show a way to overcome the dichotomy of human history. Under his cross of hope, we can envision another world, and we can act to change our societies through overcoming violence, building peace, and working for reconciliation.[43] Archbishop Desmond Tutu once said that "true reconciliation is never cheap, for it is based on forgiveness, which is costly. Forgiveness in turn depends on repentance, which has to be based on an acknowledgement of what was done wrong, and therefore on disclosure of the truth."[44]

What Tutu said in the particular context of the reconciliation process immediately after apartheid in South Africa speaks to us universally and is relevant in the global context as well. Although these words have a universal appeal, they have a local application at the same time. The people of God are called not only to listen to this message but to preach it, to live it, and to apply it in their missionary endeavors to construct peace and reconciliation.

41. "A Letter," 324.

42. Koyama, *Mount Fuji and Mount Sinai*, 44.

43. Kobia, "The Role of Religion," 2. The WCC launched the Decade to Overcome Violence (DOV) in 2001. The WCC urged churches and related organizations to unlock their spiritual resources and to address violence in their communities and in our world. The Decade sought to be a worldwide movement to confront the scourge of violence at all levels—from abuse within the family to ethnic conflict in society, form wars between countries to nuclear proliferation.

44. Tutu, Response.

CONCLUSION

Mission is participating in God's plan and work to save the whole *oik-oumene*. We are called as coworkers for this glorious task as the people of God and disciples of Jesus Christ. Our missionary mandate is to be servants preparing the feast of life and messengers inviting all God's peoples to this fiesta. It is urgent for all mission actors to introduce or reintroduce this life-centered missiological paradigm in re-visioning a new ecumenical movement in the twenty-first century. For this sake, I argue for a new foundation of mission as an invitation to the feast of life focusing on hope, spirituality, interfaith cooperation, and peace and reconciliation. Our mission is following the way of Jesus Christ, who said, "I have come that they may have life, and may have it in all its fullness" (John 10:10).

new methods
new voices
new agenda

Concluding Reflections

Stephen B. Bevans and Katalina Tahaafe-Williams

WHAT HAS CONTEXTUAL THEOLOGY *to offer the church of the twenty-first century?* This is the question with which the conference at United Theological College grappled, and to which this book has proposed some tentative answers. Naturally, the future will answer the question more fully than we ever could here, but we do think that the original conference and these eight essays have pointed very much in the right direction.

In the first essay, Stephen Bevans proposed that contextual theology in this century will offer new methods, new voices, and a new agenda. We have already seen each of these new perspectives at work in these pages.

Jione Havea's move toward what one might call a "hermeneutic of suspicion" toward contextuality itself, and his proposal of an alternative way of spelling the term—i.e., *kontextuality*—is already the employment of a fresh way of doing contextual theology. Jooseop Keum offered us a wonderful methodological image for engaging in mission in a way that respects local contexts when he suggested that Christians need to "come down from the mountain" and work with peoples of other religious ways. Although the method is not totally new, James Haire's careful study and appreciation of local cultures and languages continue to challenge contextual theologians to move beyond programmatic essays to the nitty-gritty and risk-filled work of constructing theologies that arise from a people's rich yet largely inchoate knowledge of God's presence in traditional

126

their midst. Stephen Bevans's suggestion that "prophetic dialogue" is the method for future mission work brings with it the insight that mission itself—at home or abroad—is ultimately a work of contextual theology itself. Theology here becomes reconceived as any kind of action on behalf of God's Reign—something that James Haire speaks of, as well—and points also to the fact that any theology as intellectual activity has to come from and move towards a missionary consciousness and practice. Such practice, of course, as Jooseop Keum and Jione Havea warned, cannot be based on a nineteenth-century paradigm of expansion and cultural disparagement, but on an authentic commitment to listen to, identify with, and respect the context in which mission is carried out.

Several of the authors in this volume were probably previously unknown to its readers. Carmelo Álvarez, Stephen Bevans, and James Haire have written about contextual theology for decades, but the other writers here—Chris Budden, Jione Havea, Jenny Te Paa, Jooseop Keum, and Katalina Tahaafe-Williams—are newer voices. Important, too, we believe, are the women and men with whom our authors are in dialogue, cited in footnotes and more fully in the bibliography. The rich resources used by our authors give ample evidence that, indeed, contextual theology will be alive and well in the coming decades of this century.

Finally, the essays in this book point to some of the new agendas for contextual theology in the coming decades. James Haire's is more traditional, and one that Jione Havea might disagree with, but there is, we strongly believe, the need of a construction of a solid, orthodox, and yet innovative Christology—and other traditional theological themes. This is an important task in the years ahead. Attempts at this have, sadly, been relatively few.

Jione Havea's cautions, however, are nevertheless well taken. It is not enough at all to merely translate old doctrines and ideas—the product of very particular contexts—into local language and ideas. We must start with context—or kontext—and allow the Spirit working there to reveal where God is working today. Havea's move to deconstruct some of the ordinary assumptive world of our contexts is disturbing, and yet ultimately will be a great help in the construction of new ways of envisioning Christianity. Chris Budden's project of doing theology as a Second People is one that will be useful not only for Australians, but for New Zealanders, U.S. Americans, Latin Americans, and—perhaps ultimately—many migrants and immigrants as well, *mutatis mutandis*.

Jenny Te Paa's two stories pointed to two separate yet important agendas for contextual theology today. On the one hand, a true contextual theology does indeed demand that women and men of all contexts master—or in the words of Americans James and Evelyn Whitehead, "befriend"—the tradition. Otherwise, contextual theologians are helpless in the face of some of the radical challenges that they face in their own contexts—especially when their positions are questioned and opposed by those outside of it. As Jione Havea has said forcefully, the mere demographical shift in the center of gravity of the world's population does not guarantee an equal shift in power. On the other hand, local context cannot be seen as unfailingly life giving, as Te Paa's powerful critique of the Maori warrior tradition makes plain.

Carmelo Álvarez insisted that world poverty represents a continuing agenda for liberation theology. Nevertheless, today's work for human liberation needs to focus on the importance of celebration and festivity, lest the almost impossible task lead to discouragement and burnout.

There is danger from some quarters in this twenty-first century that efforts of contextual theology will be marginalized and suppressed. Contextual theology always involves the risk of betraying the gospel, and some people in the church will think that such a risk is not worth it in the face of widespread secularism in places like Europe, North America, Australia, and New Zealand. There are certainly movements in the Roman Catholic Church to discredit any theology and pastoral practice that starts from and is measured by experience. More fundamentalist perspectives insist on adherence to particular formulas rather than creative understandings.

Our conviction in editing this volume, however, is that God's Spirit is truly working in our twenty-first-century world and is stirring up new ways of thinking about the gospel that start from women's and men's concrete experiences. The future, we know, is on the side of that great shift in the center of gravity of Christianity to the Global South. We are confident that in the years of this century, the South will indeed find its voice and discover its power. We have faith that a new catholicity is being born, one in which Christians can share their reflections-in-faith with one another—reflections, however, that emerge from new methods, new voices, and new agendas in their own contexts.

Bibliography

Abraham, K. C. "Mission as Celebration of Life." *CTC Bulletin* 24:1–2 (2008) 27–36.

Abraham, K. C., and Bernadette Mbuy-Beya, editors. *Spirituality of the Third World: A Cry for Life: Papers and Reflections from the Third General Assembly of the Ecumenical Association of Third World Theologians, January, 1992, Nairobi, Kenya*. Maryknoll, NY: Orbis, 1994.

Abraham, Susan. "What Does Mumbai Have to Do with Rome! Postcolonial Perspectives on Globalization and Theology." *Theological Studies* 69 (2009) 376–93.

Álvarez, Carmelo E. "Camilo Torres." In *Diccionario de Historia de la Iglesia*, edited by Wilton M. Nelson, 1019. Miami: Caribe, 1989.

Althaus-Reid, Marcella. "From the Goddess to Queer Theology: The State We Are in Now." *Feminist Theology* 13 (2005) 265–72.

Althaus-Reid, Marcella, Ivan Petrella, and Luiz Carlos Susin, editors. *Another Possible World*. London: SCM, 2007.

Althaus-Reid, Marcella, and Lisa Isherwood. "Thinking Theology and Queer Theory." *Feminist Theology* 15 (2007) 302–14.

Anderson, John Lee. *Che Guevara: A Revolutionary Life*. New York: Grove, 1997.

Araya, Victorio. *God of the Poor: The Mystery of God in Latin American Liberation Theology*. Translated by Robert R. Barr. Maryknoll, NY: Orbis, 1987.

Arndt, W. F., and F. W. Gingrich, editors. *A Greek-English Lexicon of the New Testament and Other Early Christian Literature*. Chicago: University of Chicago Press, 1957.

Assman, Hugo. *Crítica á lógica da exclusao: ensaois sobre economía e teología*. São Paulo: Paulus, 1994.

Barbour, Claude Marie. "Seeking Justice and Shalom in the City." *International Review of Mission* 73 (1984) 303–9.

Baretta, J. M. "Halmahera en Morotai." In *Mededeelingen van het Bureau voor de Bestuurszaken der Buitenbezittingen, bewerkt door het Encyclopaedisch Bureau*, 13. Weltevreden, Indonesia: 1917.

Barrett, David B., Todd M. Johnson, and David F. Crossing. "Christian World Communions: Five Overviews of Global Christianity, AD 1800–2025." *International Bulletin of Missionary Research* 33:1 (2009) 25–32.

———. World Christian Database. www.worldchristiandatabase.org.

Barth, Karl. *The Doctrine of the Word of God (Prolegomena to Church Dogmatics)*, Part I. Translated by G. T. Thomson. Edinburgh: T. & T. Clark, 1936.

————. *Das Evangelium in der Gegenwart*. Theologische Existenz heute 25. Munich: Kaiser, 1935.

————. "Die Theologie und die Mission in der Gegenwart." In *Theologische Fragen und Antworten*, 100–184. Zollikon: Evangelischer Verlag, 1957.

Benhabib, Seyla. *The Claims of Culture: Equality and Diversity in the Global Era*. Princeton: Princeton University Press, 2002.

Bergman, Sigurd. *God in Context: A Survey of Contextual Theology*. Aldershot, UK: Ashgate, 2008.

Bevans, Stephen B. "DB 4100: The God of Jesus Christ—A Case Study for a Missional Systematic Theology." *Theological Education* 43:2 (2008) 107–16.

————. *An Introduction to Theology in Global Perspective*. Maryknoll, NY: Orbis, 2009.

————. *Models of Contextual Theology*. Rev. ed. Maryknoll, NY: Orbis, 2002.

————. *Models of Contextual Theology*. Maryknoll, NY: Orbis, 1992.

Bevans, Stephen B., and Roger P. Schroeder. *Constants in Context: A Theology of Mission for Today*. Maryknoll, NY: Orbis, 2004.

Biéler, André. *Calvin's Economic and Social Thought*. Edited by Edward Dommen. Translated by James Greig. Geneva: WCC, 2005.

Boff, Leonardo. "Cristianismo de liberación rumbo al siglo 21." *Boletín CESEP* 19 (1994) 3–5.

————. *Ecología, mundializaçao, espiritualidade: a emergençia de un novo paradigma*. São Paulo: Attica, 1993.

Bosch, David J. *Transforming Mission: Paradigm Shifts in Theology of Mission*. Maryknoll, NY: Orbis, 1991.

Bosch, David J., J. J. Kritzinger, and Willem A. Saayman, editors. *Mission in Bold Humility: David Bosch's Work Considered*. Maryknoll, NY: Orbis, 1996.

Brett, Mark G. *Decolonizing God: The Bible in the Tides of Empire*. Sheffield: Phoenix, 2009.

Brunner, Emil. *The Word in the World*. London: SCM, 1931.

Budden, Chris. *Following Jesus in Invaded Space: Doing Theology on Aboriginal Land*. Princeton Theological Monograph Series 116. Eugene, OR: Pickwick, 2009.

Bula, Omega et al. *Reformed Faith and the Rejection of Economic Injustice: Essays on Practising the Accra Confession*. Reformed World 55. Geneva: World Alliance of Reformed Churches, 2005.

Buss, Theo. *El movimento ecuménico en perspective de teología de la liberación*. La Paz: HISBAI-CLAI, 1996.

Campen, C. F. H. "De Alfoeren van Halmahera." *Tijdschrift voor Nederlandsch Indië*. 4e serie, XII,i (April 1883) 284–97.

————. "De Godsdienstbegrippen der Halmaherasche Alfoeren." *Tijdschrift voor Indische Taal-, Land- en Volkenkunde (uitgegeven door het (Koninklijk) Bataviaasch Genootschap van Kunsten en Wetenschappen)* XXVII, Batavia (1882) 438–51.

Casaldáliga, Pedro, and José María Vigil. *Political Holiness: A Spirituality of Liberation*. Maryknoll, NY: Orbis, 1994.

Castañeda, Jorge G. *Utopia Unarmed: The Latin American Left after the Cold War*. New York: Knopf, 1993.

Castillo, Manuel, et al. *El Dios de la teología de la liberación*. Madrid: Secretariado Trinitario, 1990.

Chidester, David. *Savage Systems: Colonialism and Comparative Religion in Southern Africa*. Charlottesville: University Press of Virginia, 1996.

Chowdhry, Geeta. "Edward Said and Contrapuntal Reading: Implications for Critical Interventions in International Relations." *Millennium: Journal of International Studies* 36 (2007) 101–16.

Clements, Keith. *Faith on the Frontiers: A Life of J. H. Oldham.* Edinburgh: T. & T. Clark, 1999.

Comblin, José. *El Espíritu Santo y la liberación.* Madrid: Paulinas, 1987.

Cook, Matthew A. "Unchanging 'Truth' in Contextual Exegesis." *Evangelical Review of Theology* 31 (2007) 196–206.

Cooley, F. L. "Altar and Throne in Central Moluccan Societies." PhD diss., Yale University, 1961.

Crane, William H. "Editorial: Dropping the S." *International Review of Mission* 58 (1969) 141.

Eliade, Mircea. *The Quest: History and Meaning in Religion.* Chicago: University of Chicago Press, 1969.

Forrester, Duncan B. *Christian Justice and Public Policy.* Cambridge: Cambridge University Press, 1997.

———. "Mission in the Public Square: Christian Discourse as Public Confession." Lecture on Public Theology, University of Cambridge, June 1999. Manuscript.

Garret, J. R. *To Live Among the Stars. Christian Origins in Oceania.* Geneva: WCC, 1982.

Gathgo, Julius Mutugi. "Black Theology of South Africa: Is This the Hour of Paradigm Shift?" *Black Theology* 5 (2007) 327–54.

Gebara, Ivone. *Teología a ritmo de mujer.* Madrid: San Pablo, 1995.

Gillman, Ian, and Hans-Joachim Klimkeit. *Christians in Asia before 1500.* Ann Arbor: University of Michigan Press, 2002.

Goldman, Gerard. "Remembering Ian, Alan Goldman, and Memela: Using Narrative as an Approach to Aboriginal Reconciliation in Australia." DMin thesis, Catholic Theological Union, 1999.

Gotay, Samuel Silva. *El pensamiento cristiano revolucionario en América Latina: implicacciones de la teología de la liberación para la sociología de la religión.* Salamanca: Sígueme, 1981.

Groody, Daniel G. *Globalization, Spirituality, and Justice.* Maryknoll, NY: Orbis, 2007.

Gutiérrez, Gustavo. *We Drink from Our Own Wells.* Maryknoll, NY: Orbis, 1995.

Hadiwijono, H. *Religi Suku Murbu di Indonesia [Primal Tribal Religion in Indonesia].* Jakarta: BPK Gunung Mulia, 1977.

Haire, James. "The Centrality of Contextual Theology for Christian Existence Today." *CTC Bulletin* 24 (2008) 63–77.

Hall, Douglas John. *The Cross in Our Context: Jesus and the Suffering World.* Minneapolis: Fortress, 2003.

———. *Professing the Faith: Christian Theology in a North American Context.* Minneapolis: Fortress, 1996.

Hartenstein, Karl. *Die Mission als theologisches Problem: Beiträge zum grundsätzlichen Verständnis der Mission.* Berlin: Furche, 1933.

Havea, Jione. "The Politics of Climate Change: A *Talanoa* from Oceania." *International Journal of Public Theology* 4 (2010) 345–55.

Hayek, F. A. *Law, Legislation and Liberty.* Vol. 2, *The Mirage of Social Justice.* 2nd ed. London: Routledge, 1982.

Heim, S. Mark. *The Depth of the Riches: A Trinitarian Theology of Religious Ends.* Grand Rapids: Eerdmans, 2001.

————. *Salvations: Truth and Difference in Religion*. Maryknoll, NY: Orbis, 1995.

Heuting, A. "Geschiedenis der Zending op het eiland Halmahera (Utrechtsche Zendings-Vereeniging)." *Medeelingen: Tidschrift voor Zendingswetenschap* (Oegstgeest [The Netherlands]) 72 (1928) 1–24, 97–128, 193–214, 289–320; 73 (1929) 1–31, 97–126, 289–320; 74 (1930) 1–32, 97–128, 193–234. Subsequently published as *Geschiedenis der Zending op het eiland Halmahera*. Oegstgeest, the Netherlands: Zendingsbureau, 1935.

————. *Tobeloreesch-Hollandsch Woordenboek, met Hollandsch-Tobeloreesche inhoudsopgave*'s-Gravenhage: Nijhoff, 1908.

————. "De Tobèloreezen in hun Denken en Doen." *Bijdragen tot de Taal-, Land- en Volkenkunde van Nederlandsch-Indië (BKI)* 77 (1921) 217–358; 78 (1922) 137–n342.

————. *Van zeeroover tot christen*. Oegstgeest, the Netherlands: Zendingsbureau, 1910.

Hunsberger, George. *Bearing the Witness of the Spirit: Lesslie Newbigin's Theology of Cultural Plurality*. Grand Rapids: Eerdmans, 1998.

Jenkins, Philip. *The Next Christendom: The Coming of Global Christianity*. Oxford: Oxford University Press, 2002.

John Paul II. Encyclical Letter *Redemptoris Missio*.

Käsemann, Ernst. *Exegetische Versuche and Besinnungen*. Göttingen: Vandenhoeck & Ruprecht, 1960–64.

Keum, Jooseop. "Editorial: Evangelization of the Market." *International Review of Mission* 97 (2008) 183–86.

————. "'Take Home the Good News': The Mission of the Church in the Conext of Neo-Liberal Economic Globalization." In *World Christianity in Local Context*. Vol. 1, *Essays in Memory of David A. Kerr*, edited by Stephen R. Goodwin, 24–32. London: Continuum, 2008.

Kingsolver, Barbara. *The Poisonwood Bible: A Novel*. New York: HarperFlamingo, 1998.

Kobia, Samuel. *Called to One Hope: A New Ecumenical Epoch*. Geneva: WCC, 2006.

————. "Cooperation and the Promotion of Unity: A World Council of Churches Perspective." In *Edinburgh 2010: Mission Then and Now*, edited by David A. Kerr and Kenneth R. Ross, 237–49. Oxford: Regnum, 2009.

————. "Listening to the Voice of God: New Trends in the Ecumenical Movement." D. T. Niles Memorial Lecture. Christian Conference of Asia, April 2005. Manuscript.

————. "Report of the General Secretary: Celebrating Life—*a festa da vida*." Doc A02, WCC 9th Assembly, Porto Alegre, Brazil, February 2006.

————. "The Role of Religion in Constructing Peace and Reconciliation." Public Address, Managua, Nicaragua, November 2008.

The Kookmin Daily. Mission Session, April 2009.

Koyama, Kosuke. *Mount Fuji and Mount Sinai: A Critique of Idols*. Maryknoll, NY: Orbis, 1984.

Kruijt, A. C. "De Rijstmoeder in den Indischen archipel." In *Verslagen en Mededeelingen der Koninklijke Academie van Wetenschappen*, 361–411. Amsterdam: Afdeeling Letterkunde, Vierde Reeks, IV (1903).

Leite, Jose Correa. *The World Social Forum: Strategies of Resistance*. Chicago: Haymarket, 2004.

Libanio, João Batista. "Panorama de la teología de América Latina en los últimos veinte años." In *Cambio social y pensamiento cristiano en América Latina*, edited by José Comblin et al., 57–78. Madrid: Trotta, 1993.

Lohfink, Gerhard. *Jesus and Community: The Social Dimension of Christian Faith.* Translated by John P. Galvin. Philadelphia: Fortress, 1984.

Lossky, Nicolas, et al., editors. *Dictionary of the Ecumenical Movement.* Geneva: WCC, 1991.

Löwy, Michael. *The War of the Gods: Religion and Politics in Latin America.* New York: Verso, 1996.

Matthey, Jacques, editor. *Come Holy Spirit, Heal and Reconcile: Report of the WCC Conference on World Mission and Evangelism, Athens, Greece, May, 2005.* Geneva: WCC, 2008.

Matthiessen, Peter. *At Play in the Fields of the Lord.* New York: Random House, 1965.

Mashau, Derrick, and Martha Frederiks. "Coming of Age in African Theology: The Quest for Authentic Theology in African Soil." *Exchange* 37 (2008) 109–23.

"Mission and Evangelism: An Ecumenical Affirmation." In *New Directions in Mission and Evangelization 1: Basic Statements 1974–1991,* edited by James A. Scherer and Stephen B. Bevans, 36–51. Maryknoll, NY: Orbis, 1992.

Mitchell, Sarah. "Communitas of Christ." In *Faith in a Hyphen: Cross-Cultural Theologies Down Under,* edited by Clive Pearson, 175–84. Adelaide: Openbook, 2004.

Moffet, Samuel H. *A History of Christianity in Asia.* Vol. 1, *Beginnings to 1500s.* San Francisco: Harper, 1992.

Moltmann, Jürgen. *The Passion for Life: A Messianic Lifestyle.* Translated by M. Douglas Meeks. Philadelphia: Fortress, 1978.

Mshana, Rogate R., editor. *Alternative Globalization: Addressing Peoples and Earth.* Geneva: WCC, 2005.

Noss, John. *Man's Religions.* 5th ed. New York: Macmillan, 1974.

O'Brien, David J., and Thomas A. Shannon, editors. *Catholic Social Thought: The Documentary Heritage.* Maryknoll, NY: Orbis, 1992.

Pascoe, Bruce. *Convincing Ground: Learning to Fall in Love with Your Country.* Canberra: Aboriginal Studies Press, 2007.

Paul VI. Apostolic Exhortation *Evangelii Nuntiandi,* 1975.

Pearson, Clive, editor. *Faith in a Hyphen: Cross-Cultural Theologies Down Under.* Adelaide: Openbook, 2004.

Pedersen, Paul. *Batak Blood and the Protestant Soul: The Development of National Batak Churches in North Sumatra.* Grand Rapids: Eerdmans, 1970.

Pilkington, Doris. *Rabbit-Proof Fence.* New York: Miramax, 2002.

Raiser, Conrad. "Spirituality of Resistance." Paper presented at the WCC Internal Encounter of Churches, Agencies, and Other Partners on the World Bank and IMF. Geneva, September 2003.

Reid-Salmon, Delroy A. "A Sin of Black Theology: The Omission of the Caribbean Diasporan Experience from Black Theological Discourse." *Black Theology* 6 (2008) 154–73.

Report Evaluation Commission EATWOT. Manila: EATWOT General Assembly, 1996.

Rex, John. *Key Problems of Sociological Theory.* London: Routledge & Kegan Paul, 1961.

Reynolds, Henry. *Why Weren't We Told?: A Personal Search for the Truth about Our History.* Camberwell: Viking, 1999.

Rivera-Pagán, Luis, editor. *God in Your Grace: Official Report of the Ninth Assembly of the World Council of Churches.* Geneva: WCC, 2007.

Rudjubik, M. "Kepercayaan Agama Kafir" [Heathen Beliefs]. Kao, North Moluccas, Indonesia, 1978.

Sáez, Florencio, Jr. *Entre Cristo y el Che Guevara: historia de la subersión política en las iglesias de Puerto Rico.* San Juan: Palma Real, 1972.

Said, Edward W. *Culture and Imperialism.* New York: Knopf, 1993.

Sanneh, Lamin. *Translating the Message: The Missionary Impact on Culture.* 20th anniversary ed. Maryknoll, NY: Orbis, 2009.

———. *Whose Religion Is Christianity? The Gospel beyond the West.* Grand Rapids: Eerdmans, 2003.

Smith, Linda Tuhiwai. *Decolonizing Methodologies: Research and Indigenous Peoples.* Dunedin: University of Otago Press, 1999.

Sobrino, Jon. "The Epiphany of the God of Life in Jesus of Nazareth." In *Idols of Death and the God of Life,* edited by Pablo Richard, 66–102. Maryknoll, NY: Orbis, 1980.

———. *The Principle of Mercy: Taking the Crucified People from the Cross.* Maryknoll, NY: Orbis, 1994.

Sugirtharajah, R. S. "Introduction: Still at the Margins." In *Voices from the Margin: Interpreting the Bible in the Third World,* edited by R. S. Sugirtharajah, 1–10. 3rd ed. Maryknoll, NY: Orbis, 2006.

Suh, Jung Woon. *Spirituality and Theology in Mission: An Asian Perspective.* Seoul: PCTS Press, 2000.

Sung, Jung Mo. *Deus numa economía sem coraçao.* São Paulo: Paulus, 1992.

———. *La idolatría del capital y la muerte de los pobres.* San José: DEI, 1991.

Tamayo, Juan José. *Presente y futuro de la teología de la liberación.* Madrid: San Pablo, 1994.

"Theological Explorations into Culture." World Alliance of Reformed Churches Bali Consultation Report. *Reformed World* 38 (1985) 309–319.

Thomas, Norman, editor. *Classic Texts in Mission and World Christianity.* Maryknoll, NY: Orbis, 1994.

Thomas, P. H. "Penjebaran Agama Ksisten dan Pengaruhnja bagi Pendidikan Penduduk Halmahera" [The Spread of Christianity and Its Influence on the Education of the Population of Halmahera]. Unpublished graduate thesis, Pattimura University, Ambon, 1968.

Tobing, P. L. *The Structure of the Toba Batak Belief in the High God.* Amsterdam: Jacob Van Campen, 1956.

Turner, D. H. "Terra Incognita: Australian Aborigines and Aboriginal Studies in the '80s." Typed manuscript, 1986.

———. "Tradition and Transformation: A Study of the Groote Eylandt area Aborigine of Northern Australia." Australian Aboriginal Studies 53. PhD diss., University of Western Australia; Canberra: Australian Institute of Aboriginal Studies, 1974.

Turner, Victor. *The Ritual Process: Structure and Antistructure.* Ithaca, NY: Cornell University Press, 1969.

Tutu, Desmond. Response on his appointment as Chairperson of the Truth and Reconciliation Commission, November 1995.

Vigil, José María. "Is There a Change of Paradigm in Liberation Theology?" *LADOC* (September 1997) 7.

Walls, Andrew F. "From Christendom to World Christianity: Missions and the Demographic Transformation of the Church." In *The Cross-Cultural Process in Christian History,* 49–71. Maryknoll, NY: Orbis, 2002.

———. *The Missionary Movement in Christian History: Studies in the Transmission of Faith.* Maryknoll, NY: Orbis, 1996.

————. "Missionary Societies and the Fortunate Subversion of the Church." In *The Missionary Movement in Christian History*, 241–54.

Warren, M. A. C. Introduction to *The Primal Vision: Christian Presence Amid African Religion*, by John V. Taylor. Philadelphia: Fortress, 1963.

WCC, WARC, and CWM. "Report of *Oikotree* Consultation on Spirituality and Resistance, Liberation and Transformation." Matanzas, Cuba, May 2008.

Wiebe, Rudy. *The Blue Mountains of China*. New Canadian Library. Toronto: McClellan & Stewart, 1995.

Wijaya, Hahya. "Economic Globalization and Asian Contextual Theology." *Theological Studies* 69 (2008) 309–20.

Williamson, S. G. *Akan Religion and the Christian Faith: A Comparative Study of the Impact of Two Religions*. Edited by K. A. Dickson. Accra: Ghana Universities Press, 1965.

Willingen Conference. "A Statement on Missionary Calling of the Church." *Minutes of the Enlarged Meeting and the Committee of the International Missionary Council, Willingen, Germany, July 5–12 1952*. London: International Missonary Council, 1952.

World Missionary Conference 1910. Report of Commission VIII: Co-operation and the Promotion of Unity. New York. Revell, 1910.

World Missionary Conference 1910: The History and Records of the Conferences. New York: Revell, 1910.

World Youth Data Sheet, 2006. http://www.prb.org/pdf06/WorldsYouth2006DataSheet.pdf.

Yunupingu, Mandawuy, and Garrumul Yunupingu, composers and performers. "Gone Is the Land." On *Garma*, by Yothu Yindi. Phantom 1091333, 2007, compact disc.

1971 Synod of Bishops. "Justice in the World." In *Catholic Social Thought: The Documentary Heritage*, edited by David J. O'Brien and Thomas A. Shannon, 287–300. Maryknoll, NY: Orbis, 1992.

Notes on the Contributors

Carmelo Álvarez (Puerto Rican) is a missionary-consultant for Theological Education in Latin America and the Caribbean, Common Global Ministries Board, Christian Church (Disciples of Christ) in the United States and Canada and the United Church of Christ in the United States. He is Adjunct Professor of Church History and Theology, Christian Theological Seminary, Indianapolis, Indiana. Carmelo was ordained by the Christian Church (Disciples of Christ) in Puerto Rico. He has been a missionary in Mexico, Costa Rica, Chile, and Venezuela, 1974–1992, with his wife, Rev. Raquel Rodríguez Álvarez, an ordained pastor in the Evangelical Lutheran Church in America. He worked for twenty years in the United States as Director of Cross-Cultural Studies, Professor of Church History and Theology and Dean of Students at Christian Theological Seminary, Indianapolis, Indiana. Dr. Álvarez earned his PhD from Free University, the Netherlands, and has published fourteen books, one of them in English: *People of Hope: The Protestant Movement in Central America.*

Stephen B. Bevans (US American) is a Roman Catholic Priest of the Society of the Divine Word (SVD) and currently Louis J. Luzbetak, SVD Professor of Mission and Culture at Catholic Theological Union, Chicago. He has served as a missionary to the Philippines, 1972–1981, and has lectured and taught in many countries around the world. He is the author of *Models of Contextual Theology* (1992, 2002), *An Introduction to Theology in Global Perspective* (2009), and—with Roger P. Schroeder—*Constants in Context: A Theology of Mission for Today* (2004) and *Prophetic Dialogue: Reflections on Christian Mission Today* (2011).

Chris Budden (Australian) is a parish Minister of the Uniting Church in Australia in the Newcastle (NSW) area, an Associate Researcher with the Public and Contextual Theology Research Centre at Charles Sturt University, and adjunct faculty of United Theological College. His major research interests are justice for Indigenous peoples, and the place of people of faith in the modern, secular nation-state. His recent publications include *Following Jesus in Invaded Space* (2009) and "Acknowledging First peoples in Christian worship in Australia" in Stephen Burns and Anita Monro, editors, *Christian Worship in Australia* (2009). He is the editor of a special edition of *Uniting Church Studies* (2010) that considers the claims of the new Preamble to the Constitution of the Uniting Church in Australia in regard to the place of Indigenous peoples in Australia, in the church, and in relation to God.

The Reverend Professor James Haire (Australian) AM, KSJ, MA, PhD, DD, DLitt, DUniv is Professor of Theology, Charles Sturt University (CSU), Canberra, Australia; Executive Director, Australian Centre for Christianity and Culture (ACC&C), CSU; Director, Public and Contextual Theology (PACT) Strategic Research Centre, CSU; Past President, National Council of Churches in Australia (NCCA); Past President, Uniting Church in Australia (UCA); and a Member of the Executive and General Committees of the Christian Conference of Asia (CCA).

Jione Havea (Tongan) was baptized in the Methodist Church, and is currently Senior Lecturer in Biblical Studies, Hebrew Bible–Old Testament at United Theological College and School of Theology, Charles Sturt University (Australia). He volunteers at Parklea Prison, drinks kava and plays cards at Fofo'anga (Greenacre), and recently edited *Talanoa Ripples: Across Borders, Cultures, Disciplines* (2010) and coedited *Out of Place: Doing Theology on the Crosscultural Brink* (2011).

Rev. Dr. Jooseop Keum (Korean) is the Director of the Commission on World Mission and Evangelism (CWME) of the World Council of Churches (WCC) based in Geneva, Switzerland. He is the editor of the *International Review of Mission* (IRM), an international journal for ecumenical reflection on mission thinking and practice founded by the continuation committee of 1910 Edinburgh World Missionary Conference in 1912. He served the Council for World Mission (CWM, former London

Missionary Society) as the executive secretary for Mission Programme. He studied in Presbyterian Theological Seminary in Seoul, Korea, and New College, Edinburgh, Scotland. His current research project is the relationship between church and mission after fifty years of the integration between International Missionary Council (IMC) and the WCC.

Katalina Tahaafe-Williams (Tongan) is the director of Communitas, a program of Contextual and Public Theology at United Theological College, Sturt University, Paramatta, NSW, Australia. She is a PhD candidate at the University of Birmingham in the United Kingdom and has taught and lectured widely. She has published *The Multicultural Ministry Toolkit* (with S. Ackroyd) (2005), *We Belong: Celebrating Cultural Diversity & Living Hospitality* (with W. Hudson-Roberts) (2006), *Ministry and Mission in Multicultural Contexts* (with G. Noort & J. Wootton) (2009).

Jenny Te Paa (Maori, Aotearoa New Zealand) is Principal of Te Rau Kahikatea, a constituent of the College of St. John the Evangelist in Auckland. She was the first person to complete a degree in theology from the University of Auckland, and holds the PhD from Graduate Theological Union, Berkeley, California, and an honorary doctorate in theology from Episcopal Divinity School, Cambridge, Massachusetts. She is a highly sought-after lecturer worldwide, and has published numerous articles in both secular and theological publications from many countries.